ATLANTA UNDERGROUND

HISTORY FROM BELOW

This rail spur had continued through a tunnel between the Omni
Hotel and the Omni Coliseum, before the rails were pulled up. It
roughly aligns with the embankment that Cousin John Thrasher
built for the Monroe Railroad in 1841, although all of the surrounding

ATLANTA UNDERGROUND

HISTORY FROM BELOW

JEFFREY MORRISON

Globe Pequot

GUILFORD, CONNECTICUT

Bird's-Eye View of Atlanta, 1871 (Detail)
Detail of a rendering documenting every structure in the city, facing
approximately northwest. The three points of the railroad junction are visible,
with the Western & Atlantic Railroad to the north, the Macon & Western
Railroad to the south, and the Georgia Railroad to the east. The vaulted roof
of the newly completed second Union Station straddles the tracks next to
the State Square. Below it is the Georgia Railroad Freight Depot, the only
structure in the image that remains standing. A single locomotive is depicted
traversing the Monroe Embankment, at the western leg of the railroad wye.
COURTESY OF THE LIBRARY OF CONGRESS, GEOGRAPHY AND MAP DIVISION.

Globe Pequot

An imprint of The Rowman & Littlefield Publishing Group, Inc.
4501 Forbes Blvd., Ste. 200
Lanham, MD 20706
www.rowman.com

Distributed by NATIONAL BOOK NETWORK

British Library Cataloguing in Publication Information available
Library of Congress Cataloging-in-Publication Data

Names: Morrison, Jeffrey (Historian), author.
Title: Atlanta underground : history from below / Jeffrey Morrison.
Description: Guilford, Connecticut : Globe Pequot, [2019] | Summary:
   "Atlanta Underground presents a city history through the lens of its
   buried and paved-over urban landscape. Contemporary photos of this urban
   spelunking landscape will illustrate this telling of Atlanta's history:
   how it came to be where it is, how it acquired its unique name, and how
   its colliding street grids were established"— Provided by publisher.
Identifiers: LCCN 2019021072 (print) | LCCN 2019981372 (ebook) | ISBN
   9781493043705 (hardcover) | ISBN 9781493043712 (e-book)
Subjects: LCSH: Atlanta (Ga.)—History.
Classification: LCC F294.A857 M67 2019 (print) | LCC F294.A857 (ebook) |
   DDC 975.8/231—dc23
LC record available at https://lccn.loc.gov/2019021072
LC ebook record available at https://lccn.loc.gov/2019981372

∞™ The paper used in this publication meets the minimum requirements of American National Standard for Information Sciences—Permanence of Paper for Printed Library Materials, ANSI/NISO Z39.48-1992.

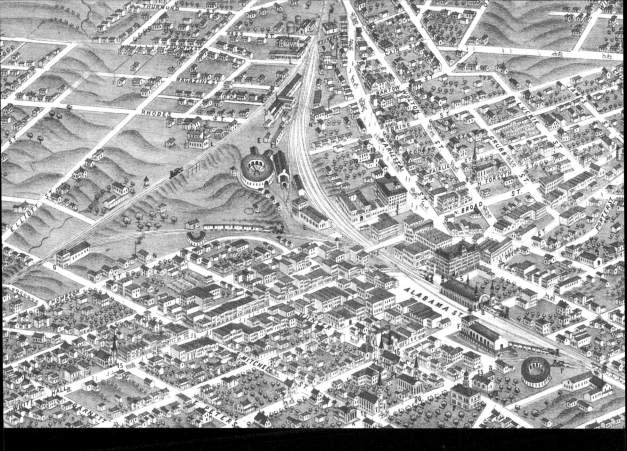

CONTENTS

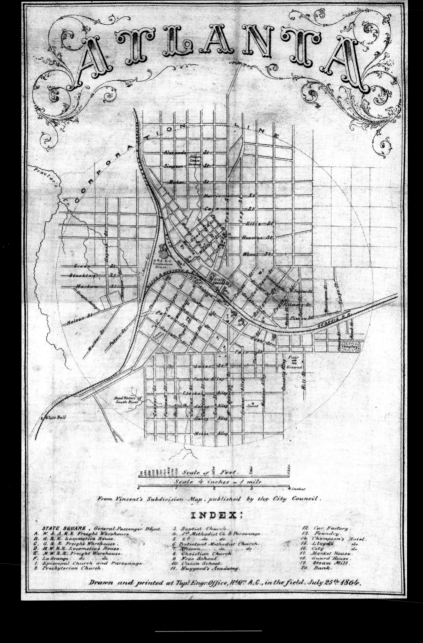

Map of Atlanta, 1864.
Map drawn by the Topographical Engineers Office of the Army of the
Cumberland on July 25, 1864, and based on Vincent's Subdivision Map of 1853.
The city limits are drawn in a one-mile radius from the State Depot. The influence
of the serpentine railroad tracks is clearly visible on the developing city street
grid, and rotated quadrants reveal the delineation of the original land lots.

To my father Andy, for always sharing
his love of trains, photography, and storytelling.

The CSX operated Western & Atlantic, beneath International Boulevard. Near this location in 1837, Stephen Long staked the terminus of the Western & Atlantic Railroad. Five years later, it was relocated to where the Zero Milepost was installed.

INTRODUCTION

DESCENDING

OUR HISTORY IS BURIED HERE. For the most part not literally underground, but unseen nonetheless. It is in the fragments of buildings embedded in the foundations of their own replacements. In reflections captured on the surface of standing water. In successive strata of urban infrastructure built upon one another. Under structures, through shadows, behind fences, out of view. Unrecognized, uncelebrated, but not forgotten. Here is the earliest history of Atlanta: how it came to be in this particular place; how it acquired its unique name; how its colliding street grids were established. It is also a record of the things that have been most important to Atlanta: transportation, growth, boosterism, and tourism. This concrete warren is where the story of Atlanta begins.

My first introduction to these spaces was unexpected. I was riding in the back seat of a friend's Honda Accord one night, darting through the streets on a shortcut between the hotels of Downtown and the artists' lofts of Castleberry Hill. Suddenly the road split, and we were on a ramp descending, or rather,

Old Magnolia Street, beneath International Boulevard. This alley ran between the Omni International Hotel and the Omni Coliseum, which was imploded and replaced with Philips Arena. It originally enclosed a railroad spur that roughly coincided with the Macon & Western Railroad's eastern leg of the triangular junction.

the rest of the road was lifting over us. A grated crescent-shaped slot in the roadway above revealed hotels lining the busy street. I sat up and my eyes widened to take in this strange new landscape. This was someplace I had never seen, never known existed.

The road descended even farther, passed under a bridge that seemed to be closed off at both ends, then through a tunnel portal puncturing a railroad embankment. Spheres of industrial halogen lights passed in a pulsating rhythm. Nearly eight stories above us, a dense array of giant concrete girders enclosed the entire space into a kind of room. To one side were stacked slabs of parking, to the other, the back side of a glowing water feature cascading down the illuminated glass-block wall of a hotel lobby. An open oversized doorway offered a glimpse into the brightly lit cavity of an enormous convention hall being prepared for an event. Broad stairways spilled out, leading nowhere. A glass-walled pedestrian bridge stretched across the chasm, but still below the false roof, with a narrow escalator suspended precariously mid-span. Circular cut-outs dotted far overhead, letting pillars of moonlight stretch down to us. It looked more like a science fiction movie set than a place for people. At the base of the Georgia Dome we turned uphill, and in less than a minute we were out on the surface streets again, squeezing between the boxy brick warehouses of Castleberry Hill.

I would return on foot many times to explore these man-made caverns. What I found was a semi-connected network of elevated streets and plazas, under which was an unplanned assemblage of alleys, parking decks, service docks, railroad tracks, stairwells, and passages. I found layers built upon layers, and the leftover spaces in between, soul-less but with the capacity for immense crowds, full of memories but unrecognizable. Quiet and immense, they appear timeless but are in fact ever-changing, forever being expanded, rebuilt, or reconfigured to some new function. The emptiness and scale feel inhuman, despite being entirely man-made, but there are also reminders of occupation on an equally grand scale: broad asphalt fields that host rowdy tailgaters, and expansive stairwells that disgorge crowds from arenas and convention halls into subway tunnels. Like a desert wash that has flooded and then dried again, these spaces are filled with an invisible history that hangs in the air.

My curiosity was piqued. I began comparing the oldest accounts of the city with the impersonal megastructures that somehow now occupied that same space. I lost myself in archives of historic photographs, but when I overlaid them with the cityscape of today, nothing matched up. In the same way that the carefully landscaped plazas at the apparent street surface offer no hint of the utilitarian complex below, there is a disassociation between this barren underworld and its rich past that is hard to reconcile.

I began to lead people through the paved-over sites of the stories I was uncovering, hoping to share with them the sense of surprise and wonder at this unexpected world hidden just beneath our feet. I called it the Unseen Underground Walking Tour. The antithesis of the tourist-laden shopping mall of Underground Atlanta, it is more of a tour of things that aren't there anymore. Of those who come, some knew this place in their youth: the excitement of arriving through Terminal Station, exploring the decrepit alleys of the old Underground, or the surreal carnival within the short-lived World of Sid and Marty Krofft. They have come to reconnect with these formative memories, and for confirmation that these missing landmarks really did exist. Other tour guests have been here for years, passing over the viaducts or looking down from the window of a sealed office tower upon this field of asphalt. They have heard references, bits of anecdotes, but have never been able to tie them to anything tangible. They have sensed a significance here, and wonder how it came to be. Some are new to Atlanta, and have come without

A commercial building suspended over the railroad is seen from
the underside. A sliver of light penetrates where the building
adjoins the sidewalk of Peachtree Street. A bolted iron bridge was
built at Peachtree Street in 1901 and replaced in 2008. Beyond
the concrete wall is the busy MARTA Five Points rail station.

State Farm Arena, formerly Philips Arena, which had been home to the Atlanta Thrashers. The hockey team did not derive its name from Thrasherville, despite playing directly above the site of John Thrasher's Monroe Embankment

judgment to better understand their new home, and indulge their fascination with the ironic struggle between past and present in a city relentlessly focused on the future.

The few remaining artifacts of that history, as significant as they are, can be difficult to find. The remnants of buildings encountered in unexpected corners raise more questions than answers. From the middle of the Central Avenue viaduct, we enter an anonymous beige-painted concrete parking garage through a windowless steel door, then walk past a bank of rusted elevators to a stairwell. It descends one level, we pass through another heavy door, then the stairwell narrows and turns in an unusual radius. We are seeking a landmark which most have heard of but few have made the effort to find. At the bottom of this stairwell, past the abandoned spiral parking ramp, through a metal gate underneath a bridge, is the actual birthplace of our city. A disturbed patch of dirt is the only sign that until recently, this was the site of an unassuming monument known as the Zero Milepost. A small stone pylon of worn and chipped granite, it was set in place in 1850 upon completion of the rail line from Chattanooga, Tennessee. Designating the southern terminus of the Western & Atlantic Railroad, it marked the point at which three railroads came together into a junction, the germ of a great metropolis in an otherwise unlikely location. It was a monument to the ignition of the city, as well as a marker of the actual center point from which the circular city limits were drawn.

Like the historic storefronts of Underground, the Zero Milepost survived beneath the streets while most everything above was rebuilt many times over. Despite its significance, it remained locked away for decades, out of view, like a precious artifact in a vault, preserved only because no one quite knew what to do with it. But the wrecking ball of progress could not be held off forever, and the Milepost was uprooted and relocated for its own protection, just before the building that had enclosed it was torn down. History is not preserved here, or celebrated, but like a ghost it lingers, and its presence cannot be denied.

One way to understand the complicated history of this area is to consider its development in terms of three stages, which could be described as nascent, classic, and experimental. In the nascent stage, the first railroads arrived and their junction became the germinating seed that created the city itself. Transportation routes were established where none had existed, populations shifted, and the city acquired a name. This period was characterized by inventiveness, entrepreneurship, optimism, and upheaval. Well-established traditions were disrupted by more modern attitudes brought on by the rapid growth of the city. This culminated spectacularly in the Civil War, and the emergence of Atlanta as the capital of the New South.

This was followed by the classic stage, epitomized by the years between the two world wars, when Downtown thrived and railroads were at the heart of everyday life. Much of the urban infrastructure that would characterize the city was built, and institutions like Rich's Department Store and the *Atlanta Journal* and *Constitution* newspapers grew in prominence. The network of railroads leading to Atlanta was completed, the great passenger stations were built, and the city streets were elevated to bridge the dense array of tracks that became the Railroad Gulch.

The destabilization of previously dependable systems, including the precipitous decline of rail traffic and the decentralization of the city's population into the suburbs, led to the experimental stage. The vacated Gulch was fertile ground for a number of bold and unexpected interventions, which could appear heroic or desperate depending on their success or failure. The nightclubs of Underground Atlanta, the Omni Complex, the massive convention center, and sports stadia would occupy much of the old railroad yards and

Parking structure beneath the Georgia International Plaza,
situated between State Farm Arena, Mercedes-Benz Stadium,
and the Georgia World Congress Center. Landscaped with lawns,
trees, fountains, and sculptures, the plaza makes for a convincing
ground plane, with few clues as to what is concealed beneath.

make the area a destination once again, but struggled to stitch together the gaps that remained. As exemplified by the audacious effort to host the Olympic Games, this is a period of transformation and reinvention that continues with contemporary visions for expansive new projects. As some of these experiments take hold, and transformation breathes new life into the city, these become the founding elements of something new.

Atlanta began as nothing more than the junction of three railroad lines, and this account is a portrait of that junction: the bustling railroad yards that developed around it, the passenger and freight depots that served it, and the viaducts built to cross over it. When Atlanta was known as the Gate City, this point where nearly all people and goods arrived and departed was that gateway. This is the story of how that junction was born, thrived, withered, and was then reimagined. This is the story of that gap in the urban fabric that would become known as the "Railroad Gulch," a dense industrial complex that held the city at bay while sustaining it, and then became equally inhospitable once abandoned by the railroads and paved over. If Atlanta has been accused of having "no *there* there," this is the "there" that isn't there. It is a wound, partially filled with monumental arenas, acres of parking, and unusual tourist attractions, but never really healed. This is an introduction to this place that has been at the core of our city since its inception, and how it has helped to make us who we are. This is the story of Atlanta, from below.

Bird's-Eye View of Atlanta, 1892 (Detail).

A second aerial rendering depicting Atlanta from nearly the same imagined vantage point as that of twenty-one years prior. Iron truss bridges cross the railroad tracks in several places. More tracks have been added inside the triangular wye to serve the full-circle roundhouse of the Western & Atlantic Railroad. The track along Elliott Street, which will eventually mark the western edge of the Gulch, has recently been added. COURTESY OF THE LIBRARY OF CONGRESS, GEOGRAPHY AND MAP DIVISION.

I THE ORIGINS OF TERMINUS

(1814–1865)

ALL THROUGH THE SUMMER OF 1864, the Union army bore down on Atlanta. They had arrived from the north, having crossed the Tennessee River near Chattanooga in the dead of night, and boldly taken Lookout Mountain under the cover of fog. Through the winter, sixty thousand Confederate troops under General Johnston held off one hundred thousand Federal troops in a series of battles at the north Georgia border, then were relentlessly driven back in successive defeats at Resaca, Pickett's Mill, and Kennesaw Mountain. The line of their assault followed the tracks of the Western & Atlantic Railroad, which was providing support to the Confederate lines from the south. From Atlanta came a steady supply of men, food, and munitions, and in turn it received wounded Confederate soldiers and captured Union troops. It also had machine shops, foundries, and railroad shops to support the army and cotton and woolen mills in nearby Roswell produced uniforms.

Union General Grant's instructions to Sherman had been to "get into the interior of the enemy's country as far as you can, inflicting all the damage you can against their resources." The thoroughness with which Sherman would fulfill this order would prove to be devastating. While he endeavored to destroy fortifications, mills, and farmlands, the railroads he sought to control—railroads that were vital to the economy of the South, linking the ports of Savannah, Charleston, and Mobile with the manufacturing centers of Richmond and Atlanta, and the agricultural regions in between. These train lines not only transported troops and supplies to the front lines, but also brought raw materials to mills that produced uniforms and weaponry. As the Union army advanced, they claimed railroads to become their own supply lines to the North. A relatively new addition to the landscape, this network of railroads led General Sherman directly to Atlanta at its hub.

In one desperate act of sabotage, a band of two dozen Union spies led by James Andrews infiltrated into Confederate territory north of Atlanta, stole a train pulled by the locomotive *General* from the depot at "Big Shanty" and sped northward, intending to destroy bridges and tracks as they went. They were thwarted by circumstances, weather, and a tireless conductor determined to retrieve his train. Captain Fuller ran after his train on foot for two miles until he reached a handcar, which he manually pumped several more miles to the nearest locomotive that could be commandeered, switched that for the next locomotive he encountered, and continued the pursuit. The Andrews Raid, otherwise known as the Great Locomotive Chase, ended ineffectually when they literally ran out of steam. Andrews and his raiders were caught and hanged, and some became the first ever recipients of the Congressional Medal of Honor. Both sides would elevate the adventure to legendary status, and it underscored the critical role the railroads held as a military asset during the Civil War.

The tracks of CSX Transportation, where originally the Georgia Railroad
met those of the Western & Atlantic. Also the site of the Union Stations
built in 1854 and 1871. Before the MARTA tracks were added with their
electrified third rail (unseen to the right), visitors to Underground could
walk across the tracks to visit the Zero Milepost, just to the left. The near
track also served as the loading platform for the New Georgia Railroad

It took two months for the Federals to reach the Chattahoochee River, but they crossed unopposed on July 8. Johnston himself retreated across the river the following day, burning the railroad bridge behind him so it could not serve as a supply line for the enemy. Within a week he had been removed from command by President Jefferson Davis, and replaced by General Hood.

Hood managed to finally halt the advancing Union army on the outskirts of Atlanta, intending to utilize a ten-mile ring of hastily constructed earthen embattlements that encircled the city. For thirty-six days, the Union armies lobbed artillery over the fortifications. Wooded hillsides were stripped bare. Brick plantation houses were riddled with holes. Although it transpired as a series of battles, for the three thousand civilians who remained in the city, it felt like a siege. All they could do was hide, and wait.

Meanwhile, the Union forces conducted a series of movements to the southwest and southeast, where they intercepted the three other railroads that served Atlanta. To the east, the Battle of Atlanta was fought along the Georgia Railroad, which ran east to Augusta and then on to Charleston. Militarily it was considered a draw, because neither side gained significant ground from where they had started, but General Sherman had succeeded in taking the railroad out of operation. Other battles cut off the Atlanta & West Point, which ran southwest toward Mobile on the Gulf of Mexico. The last line operating into Atlanta was the Macon & Western, which ran south to Macon and then connected to Savannah. It was finally taken at the Battle of Jonesboro, and the Confederates in Atlanta were left without hope of reinforcements of troops, munitions, or food.

General Hood was forced to abandon Atlanta, and evacuated all troops via the McDonough Road south to Lovejoy's Station. What they could not take with them in their retreat, they destroyed, lest it be used against them in the future. This included an entire eighty-one-car train loaded with ammunition, stranded by the severed railroad lines, which was set alight. The ensuing explosions leveled the adjacent Atlanta Rolling Mill and were felt twenty miles away in Jonesboro. The city was looted, structures were burned, and steam locomotives were rendered inoperable, before Sherman even arrived. On September 2, Mayor James Calhoun surrendered the city to Federal troops, and Sherman ordered the exile of the remaining civilian population.

The last train to leave Atlanta could only take passengers as far as Rough and Ready, the first stop south on the Macon & Western. With what little possessions they could carry, the weary survivors gathered at the Union Depot. Constructed in 1854, the Union Depot was a stout structure, grand in its simplicity. Two long walls of brick arches supported a barrel-vaulted roof. Four tracks ran through the open-air structure, flanking a central platform, on which stood a ticket office and waiting rooms adorned in the noble Italianate style. Its sister had been erected in Chattanooga at the other end of the Western & Atlantic Railroad. Also known as the "car shed" because the roof extended over the tracks, it was officially named Union Depot because it served trains from multiple railroads.

The depot stood next to the State Square, an open parcel that until recently had been filled with wounded soldiers laid out in triage, waiting to be transported to the hospitals in Newnan or Marietta. Within days, the Union Depot and much of what remained of the city would be reduced to rubble and ash. As they fled a city that appeared to be meeting its end, it is unlikely that any took note of a small stone pylon that stood just beyond the eastern portals of the depot, or to reflect upon how that pylon, the depot, or the city itself came to be there in the first place.

That stone obelisk, a railroad milepost, was in many ways the reason the entire city had come into existence. The story of how it came to be in that

Union Depot, 1864.
The scene southeast of Union Depot in the final days of the occupation of Atlanta by the Union army. The brick depot, also referred to as the Car Shed, with its vaulted roof and stout brick arcades, would be leveled within weeks. The railcars were useless to evacuees, as all railroad lines leading out of the city had been cut

The tracks of CSX Transportation beneath the CNN Center. Originally
the Western & Atlantic leg of the junction wye, and later the northern
reaches of the trackage for the third Union Station. The railroad is still
owned by the State of Georgia and leased to CSX. In the distance
is the approximate location at which Stephen Long drove a stake
indicating the terminus of the Western & Atlantic Railroad.

exact location began about three decades earlier and roughly fifty miles to the south.

It began when Mr. Sam Mitchell, a man of some prominence in the growing town of Zebulon, Georgia, took a weary traveler into his home, as was the custom. The traveler, Mr. Benjamin Beckman, worried that his horse was becoming too old or too weak to continue the journey much longer, and proposed a trade with one of Mr. Mitchell's horses that he had been admiring. To make up the difference in the value of the two horses, Beckman offered to add one of the few possessions he carried with him: the deed to a plot of land. Identified as Land Lot 77, equal to 202.5 acres, he had acquired it in 1821 in a land lottery, following the Creek cession of all their territory between the Flint and Chattahoochee Rivers.

Between 1805 and 1833, Georgia had expanded its territory westward by successively annexing land "ceded" by the indigenous Native Americans. Each time, the land had been surveyed into a grid of land lots of approximately two hundred acres, and distributed by means of a land lottery. For only a few dollars, eligible citizens, or "fortunates," had the opportunity to acquire a plot of land randomly situated on the farthest frontier. The expressed intent of these lotteries was to draw settlement westward into the most remote wilderness, far from established agricultural areas or trade centers, and to establish a presence of white settlers in land recently vacated by Native Americans. Beckman's land was an otherwise unremarkable tract of wooded rolling hills, previously occupied by the Creek Indians, not far from where the Chattahoochee River marked the boundary between the State of Georgia and the Cherokee Nation.

Mitchell accepted the offer of the aging horse and the land lot deed in exchange for his own horse, Mr. Beckman continued on his journey and was lost to obscurity, and Mr. Mitchell likely wondered if he had gotten the bad end of the deal. That is, until, in 1837, Stephen Long ceremoniously drove a stake into the ground just three hundred feet outside the limits of Land Lot 77. That stake marked the termination of the Western & Atlantic Railroad.

■

THE WESTERN & ATLANTIC WAS NOT THE FIRST RAILROAD BUILT IN THE SOUTH. In October of 1833, a train called *The Best Friend of Charleston* had arrived in Hamburg, South Carolina, having traveled the 136 miles from Charleston on the South Carolina Canal and Rail Road. The wood-burning locomotive was an awkward four-wheeled contraption with a tall vertical boiler and an open platform for the fireman and engineer. Of its initial six-mile run from Charleston, the city's newspaper, the *Charleston Courier* remarked, "The one hundred and forty-one persons flew on the wings of wind at the speed of fifteen to twenty-five miles per hour, annihilating time and space . . . leaving all the world behind. On the return . . . darted forth like a live rocket, scattering sparks and flames on either side . . . and landed us all safe at the Lines before any of us had time to determine whether or not it was prudent to be scared." It was a technical marvel at the time, the first generation of a machine that would be continuously enlarged and perfected over the following 120 years. Other railroads were being built in England and New England, but upon its completion, the South Carolina Canal and Rail Road was the longest in the world and hosted the first regularly scheduled passenger service. What made Hamburg, South Carolina, of all places in the world, such an important destination, was that it was deep within the agricultural region, across from Augusta on the banks of the Savannah River. Goods and materials that would otherwise travel to and from Savannah by boat could now be more efficiently transported by rail to Charleston. The railroad was an extension of the competition of the two rival seaports.

While extensive networks of canals were being developed in New England and Europe to transport freight cross-country, the relatively long distances between destinations and the shallowness of rivers made the railroads particularly well suited for the South. A survey expedition studied a route for a canal connecting the Tennessee River and the Chattahoochee, but found it to be impractical given the mountainous terrain and the difficulties of making the Chattahoochee navigable. Several fledgling railroads were already being constructed by private companies scattered around the state, uncoordinated and unconnected. The Central of Georgia was building westward from Savannah toward Macon, the Monroe Railroad northward from Macon to Monroe, and the Georgia Railroad from the endpoint of the South Carolina Railroad in Augusta, westward toward Athens. With the success of the South Carolina Railroad, it was tempting to envision a railroad connecting all the way from the Atlantic seaports to the Tennessee River system. And it was at this point that leaders in Georgia set forth a plan to ensure that such a connection should be made through their state, and not bypass it to the north.

In 1836, the State Assembly of Georgia established a charter for a railroad to be constructed by the state. It was to be called the Western & Atlantic Railroad, signifying the vision of connecting the Atlantic coastline with the Midwest, but in its early years it was often referred to simply as the State Road. It would begin at Ross's Landing on the banks of the Tennessee River, now Chattanooga, then wind its way through the low plateaus that make up the southern end of the Appalachian Mountain range, cross the Etowah and the Chattahoochee Rivers, and then stop. The serpentine route crossed the portion of the state which would require the most challenging engineering, and which had most recently been vacated by the Native Americans.

The railroad was intentionally built as half of a railroad, one critical leg of a future network of connecting routes. Its stated intention was to spur the development of other privately built railroads, to provide a connecting point for them to build toward, drawing them deeper into the newly settled northwestern regions of the state. Notably, the goal of the project was not to reach an existing town as its destination, although there were several in the vicinity. The cities of Decatur and Lawrenceville had both been "on the map" for over ten years. Instead, the charter simply dictated that the railroad cross the Chattahoochee and terminate at a point suitable for a junction. What might become of that junction in the future was of little concern.

A preferred location was selected for crossing the Chattahoochee River near Bolton, after studying a several-mile stretch upstream (which would have led to any number of alternate futures). The route then continued southeast until it intercepted the almost indistinguishable ridge that defines the southeastern continental divide. Separating waters that flow by way of the Flint River to the Atlantic Ocean from those that flow via the Chattahoochee ultimately to the Gulf of Mexico, the low east-west ridge would later be used as a convenient right-of-way for the Georgia Railroad to reach the same point. Beyond that, it is hard to determine how Long settled upon the particular route to follow for six miles after crossing the river, or where exactly to stop. While many factors influenced the placement of that final survey stake, its precise location, which would ultimately be so significant, seems arbitrary in retrospect.

■

THE LOCATION CHOSEN FOR THE JUNCTION was mostly wilderness, but not entirely unoccupied. During the War of 1812, in which the local Cherokee tribes fought with the British against the Americans, a loose line of wooden defensive

These tracks were built along Elliott Street in 1890 as a new western leg of the triangular junction. The tunnel penetrating the earthen embankment is Magnolia Street. The superstructure above carries Andrew Young International Boulevard and Georgia International Plaza, punctuated by circular openings to provide light and ventilation.

forts were built along the border of the Cherokee Nation. Fort Daniel occupied "Hog Mountain" in what is now Gwinett, and Fort Gilmer was built at the confluence of Peachtree Creek and the Chattahoochee River, directly across from a significant Cherokee settlement. The village was named Standing Peachtree, although accounts differ as to the proper origin of the name, even among those who manned the fort. According to one story, the village was named for a dominant peach tree of the red "Indian Blood" variety that stood atop a hill where the bodies of water met. Another attributes it to a derivation of "Pitch Tree," referring to the loblolly pine tree whose sap, or pitch, was used to seal dugout canoes. Regardless of the uncertainty of its origin, the village lent its name to Peachtree Creek, and the fort became known as Fort Peachtree. The road leading from there thirty miles to Fort Daniel was the Peachtree Road, and much of its route still bears that name today. And ultimately the moniker would be applied to hundreds of streets and parkways, as well as neighborhoods and cities. While the name has proliferated, the actual site of Fort Peachtree has been largely forgotten. Since the 1930s, it has been the site of a sprawling sewage treatment facility and the Atlanta Water Works river intake pumping station.

A branch of the Peachtree Road continued south along a low ridge to where it joined the Sandtown Trail. An establishment there named White Hall Tavern served as an inn and stagecoach stop, on what would become Whitehall Street in West End. A man with the unlikely name of Hardy Ivy is credited as being the first resident of the area that would become downtown Atlanta. But Ivy himself had moved to the area to join his in-laws, the Todd family, who had settled ten years prior, and whose nearby farm would eventually be overtaken by the Virginia Highland neighborhood. (A tiny portion of Todd Street, which led from their land to the Hardy Ivy homestead, still exists today. A marker of their family cemetery plot survived in a private backyard until 2015.) James Montgomery also lived near Fort Peachtree, where he had previously served, manning a

Beneath the Spring Street viaduct, between the site of
Terminal Station and the former US Post Office. The structure
still shows the imprint of the individual boards used to form
the concrete, and even in this utilitarian space, beams had
graceful arches and columns were given decorative capitals.

post office and operating Montgomery's Ferry across the river. Neither Ivy nor Montgomery would live to see it become the City of Atlanta.

Not far from where Long's survey had terminated, four ancient native trails that followed meandering topographical features came together. The city's first streets would be built on these trails: Peachtree Street, Marietta Street, Whitehall Street, and Decatur Street. With the later addition of Edgewood Avenue (originally Line Street, following the northern edge of Land Lot 77), they made the Five Points intersection, which would become the nucleus of the downtown business district.

When it came time for the railroads to lay out their junction, they described a triangle of broad, sweeping curves that connected the lines converging from three directions, dictated by engineering requirements, topography, and the turning radii of trains. Superimposed across the geometries of both the railroads and the wagon trails was the abstract grid of the square land lots, oriented to the cardinal directions. As land was developed within each land lot, some streets ran parallel to those emanating from Five Points, some rotated to fit along the railroad tracks, while others were aligned north-to-south with the land lot. Each arrangement was expanded upon independently until four distinct street grids developed in each of the four land lots proximate to the junction and Five Points. According to Jonathan Norcross, the commissioners appointed to oversee the planning of the city streets in a regular fashion did not exercise their duties because "they did not think it a matter of much importance . . . There were only a few that believed there would ever be a town here at all . . . and so every man built upon his own land just as he pleased." The location of the land lot boundaries is still evident where each rotated grid intersects with the next, with few, if any, continuous streets. This explains why a city with no winding waterfront or medieval warren can have such disorienting discontinuities in its street pattern.

At some point, Sam Mitchell became aware that his Land Lot 77 was no longer an anonymous tract of wilderness. The terminus point that Stephen Long had surveyed lay just east of his property. It was at the northern end of the curved triangular junction (roughly beneath what is now the CNN Center), where the Monroe Railroad intersected the Western & Atlantic. The state intended to relocate the end of the line to a spot better suited for the erection of a depot and railroad shops and approached Mitchell about extending the right-of-way onto his property. Mitchell agreed and, furthermore, donated five acres of land for the Union Depot and the adjacent State Square, recognizing the lucrative potential for the remainder of his land. With that deal, in 1842 the endpoint of the Western & Atlantic Railroad was moved twelve hundred feet to its final location, where the stone milepost would later be set beside Central Avenue between Wall and Alabama Streets. The point would also become the geographic center-point of the city. When the original city limits of Atlanta were delineated in 1847 as a perfect circle, they were described as a one-mile radius anchored about the Zero Milepost.

Having been negotiated through a horse-trade and a land-swap with the state, Mitchell's lot was perfectly positioned to take advantage of the growth of a commercial district adjacent to the Union Depot. Eventually his land would encompass such landmarks as the Kimball House hotel, Peachtree Arcade, and the businesses of Alabama Street that would later become Underground Atlanta. Perhaps this was a fitting start for a city that would be known for a spirit of boosterism and business deals. Most recently, this land was subject to yet another deal. The parking lot that had been the site of the long-lost Union Depot was transferred from the state to the city, in exchange for the pastoral acreage of Bobby Jones Golf Course on Northside Drive. The city then sold the land to a private development group that had also purchased the adjacent blocks of Underground Atlanta, in the hopes of initiating a new stage of growth for the area.

■

WHILE CONSTRUCTION OF THE WESTERN & ATLANTIC BEGAN at Ross's Landing and proceeded southward, the first work in the area of the junction was conducted by the Monroe Railroad, which was building north from Macon. To make their connection forming the west leg of the triangular "wye," it was necessary to build an earthen embankment across some low terrain. "Cousin" John Thrasher was engaged in 1839 to lead this effort, and the workforce he

Zero Milepost of the Western & Atlantic Railroad
Granite posts were set at every mile of the Western & Atlantic Railroad upon its completion in 1850, indicating the distance in each direction to the endpoints at Atlanta and Chattanooga. The opposing side reads "W&A 138." It also served as the center point of the original circular city limits.

assembled referred to their informal camp colloquially as Thrasherville. The store of Johnson & Thrasher at Five Points was the first commercial business.

For nearly a hundred years, the Monroe Embankment was technically the oldest surviving man-made structure in the city, until it was gradually subsumed as the surrounding area was filled in with dirt to lay more yard tracks.

At the same time, the area was identified informally on maps as "Terminus," because it was thought of as literally nothing more than the end of the line. The moniker exemplified the fact that, in the absence of any port, river, or significant geographical feature, it was not thought of as the location for a city.

By 1842, there were enough residents to demand a post office, and the locale was given the name Marthasville, incorporated as the Town of Marthasville a year later. The town was small enough that, rather than walking his rounds, postmaster George Washington Collier could stand on the porch of his wood-framed store at Five Points and call out names to hand out the mail individually to residents. The town boasted a primitive one-room jail made of wood that was so ineffective, that it was occasionally lifted off its foundations by prisoners to escape.

It had been proposed to name the town in honor of former governor Wilson Lumpkin, who had been instrumental in the development of the Western & Atlantic. But Lumpkin declined, already having both a county and a town that bore his name,, and so it was instead named for his daughter Martha. That, however, did not gain much favor among the locals. It was still a town of frontiersmen, railroad work gangs, and intrepid entrepreneurs. The name Marthasville was too dainty, or too sophisticated, and one can only imagine the locals referring to themselves as Marthasvillians. By comparison, the next stop south of town on the Macon & Western Railroad, during the Civil War, was called Rough and Ready. Named for a tavern, Rough and Ready was eventually incorporated as Mountain View in 1956 but had its charter revoked after only twenty-two years that were fraught with intense political corruption, a notorious freeway speed trap, and the promotion of liquor sales in an otherwise dry county. The town was then bulldozed entirely because it lay just east of the runways of Hartsfield-Jackson Atlanta International Airport, and the noise levels had made the area completely uninhabitable.

When construction of the Georgia Railroad was completed to Marthasville in 1845, its superintendent, Richard Peters, sought a more fitting name for his railroad's new destination. His chief engineer, J. Edgar Thompson, proposed "Atlanta," although it is not clear exactly what inspired him. A coined word, appropriate for a city generated out of nothing, it was strong, aspirational, and vaguely classical. He suggested that it was the feminine form of "Atlantic," commemorating the terminus of the Western & Atlantic Railroad. It appealed to Peters, perhaps because of the symmetry of the Georgia Railroad running from Augusta to Atlanta, or maybe even recognizing a parity between the new inland junction and the ports on the Atlantic coast. Some accounts suggest that it was shortened from a more grandiose but unwieldy "Atlantica-Pacifica." Contrary to local lore, it had no relation to Martha Lumpkin, although she was known to some as "Miss Attie." Nor was it derived from Atalanta, a virgin huntress in Greek mythology who symbolized fleetness and strength. The similarity was compelling, as high culture of the South held a strong affinity for ancient Greece and Rome, evident in the ubiquitous neoclassical architecture and the nostalgic naming of places such as Athens, Rome, and Sparta.

Rather presumptuously, the Georgia Railroad disregarded the name Marthasville and instead used Atlanta on its timetables and for the sign on its freight depot. The name caught on quickly and was soon adopted by the post office, then the state legislature made it officially the Town of Atlanta. Two years later it was rechartered as the City of Atlanta, with a mayor and city council organized, and the city limits were established as a one-mile radius from the depot. A single polling place was sufficient for the 215 votes cast, and Moses Formwalt was elected the first mayor of Atlanta for a one-year term. Formwalt was twenty-eight years of age and had only lived in Atlanta for two years, selling stills in a tin shop on Decatur Street. He represented the "Free and Rowdy Party," in opposition to the "Moral Party," and was backed by a contingent of saloon and brothel owners concentrated in the disreputable neighborhoods of Snake Nation, Slabtown, and Tight Squeeze.

■

ATLANTA WAS A RAPIDLY GROWING TOWN of merchants, carpenters, and railroad men. Within an eight-month period in 1847, 187 buildings were constructed, including thirty stores, two hotels, and two schools. Dr. William White described the frenzy of growth he witnessed upon his arrival into town: "The woods all around are full of shanties, and the merchants live in them until they can find time to build. The streets are full of stumps and roots; large chestnut and oak logs are scattered about, but the streets are alive with people and the stores full of trade and bustle. Not a church has yet been built . . . Preaching is held in the railroad depot . . . I have only been here two days and am becoming quite an old settler. The people here bow and shake hands with everybody they meet, as there are so many coming in all the time that they cannot remember with whom they are acquainted. . . ."

Meanwhile, construction of the Western & Atlantic was arduous and sporadic. All funding came from state-issued bonds, and work was stalled several times during economic downturns. The engineering obstacles along the 138 miles were significant compared to what had been attempted elsewhere. It was dubbed "the crookedest railroad in the world" because of the way it snaked its way along the contours of the many ridges that crossed its path.

Parking structure beneath Georgia International Plaza,
between the Georgia World Congress Center and Mercedes-
Benz Stadium. The deck occupies a low point in the
topography, such that the landscaped plaza at the top level
is roughly aligned with the elevation of the viaducts.

On Christmas Eve of 1842, crowds filled the State Square to cheer the departure of the first train from Atlanta to Marietta on the Western & Atlantic. A small wooded depot serving passengers and freight stood where the Georgia Railroad would later make its connection from the east. The train consisted of a boxcar and a single coach pulled by the locomotive *Florida*. When the train reached the wooden bridge that had been built across the Chattahoochee River, passengers insisted on getting out and walking across the bridge, unconvinced of its safety. As there was still no through connection in any direction, the locomotive had been hauled in from the end of the Georgia Railroad at Madison on a wagon pulled by a team of sixteen mules over sixty miles of rutted dirt roads, in what must have been a frustrating contradiction in the struggle for progress.

The last portion of the Western & Atlantic to be completed required digging a fifteen-hundred-foot tunnel directly through the solid rock of Chetoogeta Mountain. Until the tunnel's completion, trains would travel from Atlanta to the south portal of the tunnel, where passengers would disembark and climb over the mountain on foot while porters hauled their baggage. They would descend and board another train waiting on the other side that would continue them along their journey north.

The tunnel was finally opened in 1850 (now a historic attraction, having been bypassed later when the route was reengineered), and after fourteen years, the Western & Atlantic was complete. A final step was to install stone mileposts along the entire route, counting up and down each mile from Atlanta to Chattanooga, primarily to be used as reference points for maintenance crews. At the point of origin, the center of the city, near the wood depot and adjacent to the State Square, was installed the Zero Milepost, a granite post, twelve inches square with a pyramidal top, originally standing about five feet out of the ground, inscribed "W&A 00" on two sides and "W&A 138" on a third.

The Monroe Railroad, by then the Macon & Western, had been completed in 1846. An unnamed resident recalled that "This was the time that the first railroad whistle was ever heard in Atlanta. The engines on the Georgia and W. & A. railroads were little fellows without any whistles. But the engine on the Macon road had a real whistle, and it made a great stir when it was first heard in Atlanta." The design of steam trains had in twenty years been considerably refined, and the locomotives had taken on their familiar, if antique, nineteenth-century appearance. A few miles south of town, the Atlanta & West Point branched off toward the southwest. Completed in 1854, it spanned between the aptly named cities of East Point and West Point, on the Alabama border, where it connected to the Montgomery & West Point Railroad to Montgomery. Twenty years after the charter of the Western & Atlantic, the vision was fulfilled. Atlanta stood at the hub of a network of rail lines that spanned the South, connecting the eastern seaports from Richmond to Savannah, and Gulf ports of Mobile and New Orleans, to inland river towns of Chattanooga, Nashville, and Memphis.

In 1853 Atlanta was made the county seat of the newly formed Fulton County, named in honor of Hamilton Fulton, a surveyor and engineer for the state. Fulton is credited with making the assessment that a transportation route through the area would be best constructed as a railroad instead of as a canal. A structure to serve as both city hall and county courthouse was built on a small rise overlooking the junction, which would eventually become the site of the state capitol. As a commercial core developed between Five Points and the Union Depot, the streets were illuminated by the installation of fifty gas lamps, installed and operated by the Atlanta Gas Light Company, which is now the city's oldest surviving corporation. Mayor William Ezzard coined

The Spring Street viaduct, completed in 1923. The bridge was replaced in 2016, part of an initiative by the Georgia Department of Transportation to incrementally replace all of the historic viaducts with modern structures.

the name "the Gate City" in 1857, when the completion of the Memphis & Charleston Railroad created the first continuous rail connection between the Mississippi River and the Atlantic by way of the Western & Atlantic. He proclaimed Atlanta as "The Gate City, the only tribute which she requires of those who pass through her boundaries is that they stop long enough to partake of the hospitality of her citizens."

This network of railroads fueled the economy of the South, and during the Civil War became the engine for its war machine. After being relatively insulated from the battlefields of Virginia, Maryland, and Pennsylvania for the first several years of the war, it became clear that Atlanta lay on the path to defeating the Confederacy. The junction, Atlanta's greatest asset, became a military target, and the railroads became a path leading directly to it.

■

AFTER OCCUPYING THE CITY FOR TWO MONTHS, Sherman ordered the destruction of Atlanta in preparation for his departure. The railroad depot was destroyed, as were the roundhouse and railroad shops, and adjacent businesses in the heart of the city. The bridge across the Chattahoochee River, which had been repaired for their use, was again destroyed. This cut off Sherman's army from the North, but further ensured that Atlanta could not be reestablished as a Confederate stronghold. Having left Atlanta in ruins, General Sherman proceeded on his "March to the Sea," leaving a path of total destruction eighty miles wide. Sherman's troops marched from Macon to Savannah, following the tracks of the Central of Georgia Railroad, looting, destroying houses, and burning fields. Iron rails were removed from the tracks, heated over bonfires, and wrapped around tree trunks, and referred to as "Sherman's Neckties." In December 1864, the City of Savannah fell, and was presented to President Lincoln as a Christmas present, only four weeks after he was elected to his second term in office. Confederate forces would continue to fight for several months, but their resources were entirely depleted. The end of the war was inevitable.

Civilians returned to the smoldering remains of Atlanta as soon as Sherman was gone. With just $1.64 in the city treasury, they began to rebuild. The displaced populace flooded back in and was soon joined by opportunists from the North. The population, which had actually doubled during the war to over twenty thousand, was regained by 1866. It would nearly double in the next two decades, and double again the decade after that. The official seal of the city, which had originally borne the image of a steam locomotive, was replaced with a phoenix, the mythical bird reborn from fire, its wings spread broad and head aloft. To this day, it bears the inscription "*Resurgens,*" Latin for "Rising Again," along with two dates: 1847, the year of its founding, and 1865, the year it rose from the ashes. In spite of its humble origins as Terminus, little more than a point on a survey map, nothing could prevent Atlanta from its destiny to become one of the great cities of the South.

Bird's-Eye View of Atlanta, 1919 (Detail).
The density of urban development, as well as the continued expansion of tracks within
the railroad junction, is visible in this aerial rendering. The Union Station of 1871 is barely
visible to the far right. Terminal Station is present on the west side of the junction, with the
vaulted train shed that would be dismantled in 1925. The yard tracks of the A.B.&A. are on an
embankment to the west of that. COURTESY OF THE LIBRARY OF CONGRESS, GEOGRAPHY AND MAP DIVISION

II

ARRIVALS AND DEPARTURES

(1866–1971)

THE ENGINEMEN HAD GONE TO GREAT LENGTHS to ensure that locomotive #1517 had never looked better. The black jacket was clean; the brass cylinder heads were polished. The 4-6-0 Ten Wheeler built by Baldwin Locomotive Works in Philadelphia was just a year old. The coal-filled tender bore the thin gold letters "A. B. A." It proudly pulled a short train of varnished wood private cars filled with executives from the railroad and local dignitaries. This "Atlanta Chamber of Commerce Special" was the first train to arrive in Atlanta on the newly completed Atlanta, Birmingham & Atlantic Railroad, on June 19, 1908. It was promoted as the "BEE Line" for the relatively direct route it offered for those needing to travel from Brunswick, Georgia, to Birmingham, Alabama. A branch line led from the town of Montezuma, Georgia, to Atlanta. The AB&A's expansion was led by Henry Atkinson, who also headed the Georgia Electric Light Company and had consolidated

Atlanta's electric streetcars under the Georgia Railway and Electric Company.

The occasion marked the arrival of the tenth and last railroad connecting Atlanta to all points of the compass. The train pulled in to Union Station amid crowds of press and spectators. This second Union Station had opened in 1871 on the same site as its ruined predecessor, at the meeting point of the Western & Atlantic and the Georgia Railroad, next to the State Square. Like the depot before it, it was a linear vaulted structure that spanned over the tracks, open at both ends, with ticket offices and waiting rooms along one side. It exhibited the latest trends in building technology and fashion, an eclectic Victorian composite of slate mansard roofs with pointed spires and metal filigree, on a robust cast iron structure. Each end of the arched roof had a distinctive radial sunburst pattern crowning the six tracks that entered below.

As impressive as it might have been, the depot that welcomed the AB&A had not aged particularly well in its thirty-seven years. The polychromatic exuberance of the Victorian exterior was entirely caked in black soot, and it had undergone several unsympathetic renovations. Difficult-to-maintain exterior detailing went askew, or was removed altogether. The open sunbursts at each end had been enclosed with glass panels, which only trapped in the smoke from the locomotives and made the platforms more unpleasant for travelers.

A more modern facility had already been built at the other end of the junction in 1905, with twice the capacity. The grand Terminal Station was built by the newly formed Southern Railway to serve their family of lines, which included the Seaboard Air Line, Central of Georgia (formerly the Macon & Western), and the Atlanta & West Point. The Southern Railway Company was

organized in 1894 from a collection of other railroads by Georgia native Samuel Spencer. Although headquartered in Washington, DC, the company had a significant presence in Atlanta. Terminal Station stood at the southeastern end of the junction, near John Thrasher's Monroe Embankment. Union Station remained in operation, serving the Nashville, Chattanooga & St. Louis (which had in 1890 begun leasing the Western & Atlantic), the Georgia Railroad, the Louisville & Nashville (L&N), and the Atlantic Coast Line.

Terminal Station's clay-tile roofs, rounded arches, tan brick walls and terracotta detailing exemplified the Renaissance Revival style. The four-story head house was framed by two towers capped by open-arched cupolas. In addition to ticket offices and waiting rooms, the station's amenities included a dining room, ladies cafe, men's reading and smoking room, and mail and baggage rooms. A concourse with ample skylights bridged across the tracks, with stairwells leading down to each platform. These were enclosed by a cavernous steel and glass vaulted roof 540 feet long with a clear span of 265 feet across ten parallel tracks, dwarfing the trains below. The station stood on an elevated platform that aligned with the adjacent Mitchell Street and Madison Avenue (renamed Spring Street, now Ted Turner Drive) that bridged across the railroad tracks in two directions. The station entrance was at the elevated street level, set significantly back from Spring Street, leaving an open plaza as an expansive automobile fore-court. While it was served by streetcar lines, and was certainly an optimization of railroad efficiency itself, the role of the automobile in the facility's design was foretelling.

In the 1890s, the city had allowed the East Tennessee, Virginia & Georgia Railroad (E.T.V. & G.) to lay tracks on an embankment along Elliott Street, two blocks west of the junction, to reach its new wooden depot at Mitchell Street. Shortly after, the E.T.V. & G. became part of the Southern Railway, which planned to build Terminal Station near the E.T.V. & G. depot. The

The concrete structure of the Spring Street viaduct was accented with arches and ornamental balusters, and bore the imprint of the wood boards of the formwork. Diagonal lines on the columns mark where they had once intersected the butterfly shed roofs over the boarding platforms of the third Union Station.

Elliott Street line became the new main line, and space between it and the rest of the junction was gradually filled in with expanding yard trackage. Most of Elliott Street is long gone, and the yards have long since been paved over, but the busy tracks of the modern Norfolk Southern follow that line.

■

FROM TEN DIFFERENT DIRECTIONS, RAILROADS SNAKED THEIR WAY THROUGH THE CITY toward the two passenger stations and the three points of the junction wye. A railroad wye is a triangle of track formed by three arcs that allows trains to take any divergent route or to turn around. Late-comer railroads were granted access to the city only with strict limitations, in efforts to control the competition. This resulted in another, more geometrically convoluted junction, Howell Junction, at which several lines converged before continuing south to the passenger stations. In most cases this required negotiating arrangements to operate trains on the tracks of the existing railroads to cover the last few miles into the stations. For example, trains of the Southern Railway could get as close as Howell Junction, and then had to back up into Terminal Station on the tracks of the Nashville, Chattanooga & St. Louis, which operated the old Western & Atlantic line.

Various connecting spurs, or belt lines, were built to bypass the congestion of the terminals. The main line of the Atlanta & Richmond Air-Line Railway, coming southwest from Virginia in 1873, followed Clear Creek to intersect with the Georgia Railroad just east of downtown. When it was purchased by the Southern Railroad, a branch was laid north of the city connecting over to the Western & Atlantic at Howell, so that trains could come into Terminal Station from the north. The Atlanta & West Point built a loop around the southeast side of the city to connect to the Georgia Railroad. To the west, the L&N acquired a leg built by the Atlanta, Knoxville and Northern Railway, giving the L&N access to its affiliate the Georgia Railroad without having to pass through the congested downtown. This collection of disjointed bypasses was built independently, without any intention of being used as a continuous loop, but have now been linked together as the Atlanta Beltline trail and transit corridor.

The early railroads had chosen the preferred routes, and the city had grown around them. Being the last on the scene, the AB&A had a much bigger challenge getting access to the heart of the city. Coming north, the line passed to the west of downtown, then looped around near Howell. A short connecting spur there was negotiated to get trains into Terminal Station. Otherwise, freight trains traveled along an elevated embankment that cut southeast and across the impoverished Lightning neighborhood and terminated in a large rail yard along Mangum Street, built on fill above the adjacent houses one block west of the tracks of Terminal Station. The invasive construction had required the removal of fifteen hundred homes. Eighty years later, AB&A's Terminal Yard on Mangum Street would itself be completely obliterated to make way for the Georgia Dome football stadium.

Being last to the table did not offer the AB&A sufficient rewards to pay for the expense of getting there. A year after its triumphant arrivals in both Atlanta and Birmingham, the railroad was already in receivership. In an industry where competition was fierce, and expansion was necessarily fast and costly, bankruptcies were common. Railroad names changed frequently with acquisitions and consolidations. The AB&A had originated as the Birmingham Railway in 1887, then became the Atlantic & Birmingham Railway in 1904, which changed to the Atlanta, Birmingham & Atlantic Railroad a year later. Following the bankruptcy it was restructured as the Atlanta, Birmingham &

Atlantic Railway. By 1921 it was in receivership again, to be acquired five years later by the Atlantic Coast Line and reorganized as the Atlanta, Birmingham & Coast Railroad, nicknamed the "ABC." By mid-century, the struggling industry had transitioned from proliferation to consolidation. The Atlantic Coast Line merged with the Seaboard Air Line Railroad in 1967 to form the Seaboard Coast Line, which merged with the L&N in 1982 to create the Seaboard Systems Railroad, which was then renamed in 1986 to CSX Transportation. At that point all of the railroad operations in Atlanta had been consolidated under either the CSX or the Norfolk Southern, which have continued successfully to this day.

■

ALL TEN OF THE RAILROADS THAT CONVERGED UPON ATLANTA carried passenger trains into either Union Station or Terminal Station, as well as to numerous small stations throughout the increasingly interconnected cities of the area. Each railroad had its own rail yards for switching inter-city freight trains, unloading freight for local destinations, and assembling trains. These expansive yards included roundhouses, car repair shops, machine shops, and facilities for loading coal, fuel oil, and water into the locomotives.

Much of the area within the original triangular wye had been leveled with fill dirt to make room for tracks. John Thrasher's original Monroe Embankment was gradually buried as room for new tracks was created, and was eventually subsumed entirely. After expanding two blocks west to the new track on Elliott Street, the space between was soon taken up with more parallel sidings. In addition to the two passenger stations, sidings served freight depots and warehouses that surrounded the junction, along with locomotive servicing shops and roundhouses.

Union Station, 1890.
The cast iron vault of the second Union Station is viewed from the Broad Street bridge, looking east. It was built in 1871 on the same site as the first Union Station. Buggies and carriages fill Wall Street to the left of the tracks, with the balconies and turrets of the Kimball House looming above. The train is blocking both Whitehall and Pryor Streets, a common condition which would only get worse as rail and street traffic increased. COURTESY OF THE ATLANTA HISTORY CENTER.

Travelers laden with baggage arrived and departed from the passenger stations at all hours of the day. They stayed in hotels, grand and grimy, nearby. The Kimball House filled an entire block between Union Station and Five Points. Its lavish interiors housed shops, meeting rooms, and 357 hotel rooms. Seven stories tall, it was a frenetic assemblage of turrets, balconies, and dormers that reflected the vitality of the streets that pressed against it on all sides. Restaurants, lunchrooms, saloons, and merchants served travelers and visiting railroad men. The busiest commercial streets were Alabama Street, Marietta Street, and Decatur Street, tightly framing the railroad junction. Downtown businesses crowded together to be within a short distance of the depots and each other. A steady flow of electric streetcars carried people conveniently through all parts of Downtown, whether running errands, going to work, or seeing a show. The extensive streetcar network radiated for miles into the surrounding residential neighborhoods. Tall buildings formed a nearly perfectly concentric density centered at Five Points and diminishing outward, containing an equally focused concentration of population and commerce. Freight depots and warehouses squeezed into every available space along the tracks. Goods were unloaded from lines of boxcars on stub sidings, loaded into small trucks to be distributed to businesses throughout the area, and the same process happened in reverse.

The result was an intense amount of pedestrian and vehicular traffic on the streets that crossed the tracks, which could often be blocked by increasingly long and frequent passenger and freight trains. In spite of how much they depended on one another, it soon became clear that the railroads were at odds with the surrounding city street life. Long trains waiting at the station blocked the steady flow of pedestrians, horse carts, trucks, and automobiles. The first bridge across the tracks was built at high ground, a simple wooden bridge for pedestrians built during the Civil War at Broad Street. This was replaced in 1891 with a spindly iron box-truss bridge there at Broad, and another at Forsyth. A more stout bridge of riveted steel lattice girders was built at Peachtree Street in 1901 (which would stand for over one hundred years), and by 1923 a steel and concrete bridge, trimmed with spindled cast-concrete baluster railings, spanned across the tracks from the elevated entrance of Terminal Station all the way to Marietta Street.

From the vantage point of the elevated viaducts, the railroad yards were a dirty, noisy, dangerous realm only for trains, railroad men, and hobos. The canyon-like no-man's-land framed by tall buildings and bridges on all sides came to be referred to as "the Gulch."

Development in and around the Gulch continued in an ad hoc fashion, but some people believed there was a better alternative. As the industrialized vein of iron splitting through the business district became less and less hospitable to the city dwellers, Atlanta architect Haralson Bleckley had a bold vision to transform the Gulch into a massive public amenity. The City Beautiful movement, begun in the late nineteenth century, promoted the application of master planning principles and forethoughtful design to cities which otherwise tended to grow as a conglomeration of individual decisions made one parcel at a time. Their goal was to create civic beauty, manage traffic circulation, and improve public health. They promoted public parks, tree-lined boulevards, and the earliest land-use zoning to prevent, for example, a slaughterhouse being located next to a school. Axial streets providing long vistas that terminated at civic buildings or monuments imposed order and clarity onto an otherwise disjointed network of streets. They even espoused the theory that such urban planning could improve the moral character of the residents. In America, cities such as Chicago and Washington, DC, began to implement these ideals with grand infrastructure projects, but they were more generally popularized in the increasingly elaborate but temporary buildings and grounds of fairs and expositions.

Beginning in 1881, Atlanta hosted a series of agricultural fairs intended to showcase the products of the state and promote Atlanta as the heart of the New South. These were first held west of downtown on a site later occupied by the Exposition Cotton Mills, followed by the Piedmont Exposition of 1887, held on the grounds of the Piedmont Driving Club at what is now Piedmont Park. The most spectacular of these was the Cotton States and International Exposition of 1895, also at Piedmont Park.

The event hosted more than eight hundred thousand visitors over a span of one hundred days, at a cost of two million dollars. Exhibits ranged from agriculture and manufacturing to the liberal arts, including an exotic Mexican Village, and a midway featured rides and performances by Buffalo Bill's Wild West Show. The grounds contained eighteen large buildings and dozens of smaller pavilions, a man-made lake, and landscaped grounds designed by Joseph Forsyth Johnson. All of the structures were designed specifically for the event, and torn down shortly after, but nonetheless captured the exuberance and optimism of the Gilded Age. The exposition was clearly inspired by the Chicago World's Columbian Exposition of 1893, which had created an illuminated, brightly painted "White City" out of thin air. Smooth broad streets lined with electric streetlights framed monumental neoclassical buildings that, despite being largely made of plaster, exuded strength and stability. Overall, the effect was that of an idealized city, a celebration of order, composition, civility, and graciousness. It helped that this city could ignore the more practical requirements of factories, slums, stockyards, or for that matter, government or residents. In practice, it was more often the model for amusement parks, which often claimed the moniker of "White City," rather than practical city planning.

The *Atlanta Constitution* newspaper moved into this new modern headquarters in 1947, but occupied it for only three years before merging with the *Atlanta Journal* on Marietta Street. The site beside the Gulch provided a central location for reporters and a railroad siding to serve the printing presses. The building was later purchased by the City of Atlanta but has been neglected for decades.

Likely inspired by these experiments in idealized urban design, Atlanta architect Haralson Bleckley in 1909 mapped out his own ambitious vision for downtown in a series of ink line perspective drawings. The central idea was to create a broad civic plaza capping the railroad tracks, a full block wide and extending from the State Capitol to Terminal Station. The long rectangular open space was delineated with formal gardens and geometric plazas, and spatially defined by a wall of tall buildings on either side that gave it the feeling of an outdoor room. The surrounding blocks were tightly packed with tall modern buildings. Each was a unique celebration of contemporary Beaux-Arts styling, and with just a few notable exceptions, each was the product of Bleckley's own imagination. One end of the open space was terminated by a skyscraper extending boldly above the skyline; the other was crowned with a monumental passenger terminal sitting atop the exposed edge of the platform. Dozens of train tracks spilled out from beneath the station, flaring out in the distinctive curvature of the junction wye.

Bleckley's renderings expressed an ambition to use the Gulch as an opportunity to impose a new organizing form into the jumbled downtown, to introduce an ordering concept of such singular clarity that it would focus the growth of everything around it. Bleckley pursued the project for decades, and generated broad support among the public, but it was never adopted by the city council or state legislators. The city did focus on upgrading and expanding the viaducts from 1928 to 1936, but when they finally created the first public space over the Gulch in 1949, Plaza Park, it was a tiny gesture compared to Bleckley's vision. The third Union Station was built not far from where he had imagined it, and in a similar neoclassical style, but the station was much smaller in scale, off center at an awkward angle, and opened onto little more than a wide spot in the street.

Through the twentieth century, the space above the tracks would be filled by a patchwork of commercial buildings, parking structures, and open plazas, but without any spatial integration. Regardless, the temptation to imagine a new city center capping the Gulch persists to this day.

■

AT PRECISELY 1:40 P.M. EACH AFTERNOON from 1947 until 1971, the *Nancy Hanks* arrived at Terminal Station with little ceremony but with no small amount of anticipation. The golden age of railroading was epitomized by the famous streamliners: the New York Central's stately *Twentieth Century Limited* speeding from New York City to Chicago; the Southern Pacific's *Daylight*, streaked with the colors of the sunset; or the *California Zephyr*, snaking along the Feather River Gorge on the Western Pacific. Thundering locomotives wrapped with stylized streamlining pulled matching strings of coaches with colorful paint schemes, terminated with rounded observation cars. The Southern Railway's *Crescent* and the Seaboard Air Line's *Silver Comet* passed through Atlanta on their way from New York to New Orleans and Birmingham, respectively. Other named trains stopping in Atlanta included the *Piedmont*, *Flamingo*, *Dixie Flier*, and the *Man O' War*. The *Nancy Hanks* was not necessarily glamorous, but it nonetheless holds a place of fondness in the hearts of those who rode it.

The "Nancy" ran daily on the Central of Georgia Railroad, from Savannah to Atlanta via Macon and back again, a six-hour trip each way. It was perfect for making day trips into Atlanta, filled with businessmen, housewives on shopping trips to Rich's or the Peachtree Arcade, children visiting their grandparents, and school groups on field trips. Technically the *Nancy Hanks II*, the train was named after an earlier steam train, that was named for a racehorse

Aerial Photographic Survey, 1949.
Partial photograph from a comprehensive aerial mosaic assembled of the entire city, titled "Planning Atlanta—A New City in the Making." The distinctive geometries of the rail lines are in sharp contrast to the surrounding street grids. Both Terminal Station and the third Union Station are present, their linear platform roofs filling

that was named after Abraham Lincoln's mother. The train was pulled by an E-7 diesel unit with a thin cab window mounted high over a rounded nosing, and each of the blue and white coaches bore the silhouette of the namesake horse. The train included a grill car, and in later years, a domed parlor car featuring the Saddle and Stirrup lounge.

Approaching slowly from the south, the *Nancy Hanks* rolled past the signals that confirmed its entry into the yard limits, under the bridges for Peters Street, Nelson Street, and Mitchell Street, and past the sidings worming between the warehouses of Castleberry Hill. It passed the South Interlocking Tower, a small two-story structure set amidst the tracks from which the turnouts and signals were controlled. One such tower was positioned at each of the three points of the junction, controlling all the traffic that passed through. In 1927, near the peak of rail travel in the United States, there were 326 passenger train arrivals and departures combined between the two stations, carrying over ten thousand passengers through Atlanta every single day. In addition to that there were dozens of freight trains, most of which passed through the junction en route to the nearby freight yards.

From his vantage point in the tower, the yard master had a commanding view of the yard tracks, signals, and trains. It was a tiny two-story structure with one room on each level connected by an iron spiral staircase. The upper level was wrapped with windows on all four sides, giving a panoramic view of the many tracks leading into Terminal Station from the south. Built at the same time as Terminal Station, it exhibited the same tan brick, terra-cotta roof tiles, and a round brick-arched doorway. The tower at the north point of the yard was its twin.

The dispatcher mapped out routes for each train movement through the maze of yard tracks and issued his instructions as train orders, and the yard master in the tower was responsible for making sure that each train was directed onto the appropriate track. A densely packed row of shoulder-high levers was lined up below the windows, each requiring two hands and a foot to operate. The levers operated the turnouts that needed to be aligned, as well as the signals mounted over the tracks that indicated to the locomotive engineers that the route was clear. The "interlocking" mechanisms ensured that turnouts could not be set in such a way as to allow conflicting train movements. Prior to the implementation of radios, the complex choreography of train arrivals and departures was only possible through strict adherence to time schedules. In time, the mechanical levers were replaced with electronic controls and motorized turnouts. Telegraphs were replaced with radio communications and eventually satellite GPS tracking. Now all train dispatching for the entire Norfolk Southern Railroad is conducted remotely from a single location.

A large central post office was built across from Terminal Station in 1933. It was clad entirely in white Georgia marble and designed in an early art deco style that would later exemplify projects of the Works Progress Administration. The US Postal Service operated a railway post office (RPO) car at the head end of most intercity passenger trains. A tunnel beneath Spring Street provided a direct passage for hauling mail from the passenger terminal platforms to the basement of the post office. Inside the cramped RPOs, postmen collected, sorted, and redistributed mail to towns along the train route. Ensuring that mail addressed to an upcoming town was ready in time was a complicated and demanding task, often performed while traveling at speeds of seventy miles per hour or more. At smaller depots, if the train did not have a scheduled stop, the outgoing mail bag was hoisted onto a gantry alongside the tracks, and as the train sped past at full speed, a hook mounted on the car grabbed the bag and pulled it into the RPO. Simultaneously, the arriving mail bag was tossed from the train onto the station platform to be retrieved. The timing of this exciting exchange was critical.

The RPO was one of the things that made the railroads so important to the daily life of Americans, and also served to subsidize passenger trains. Nearly every community was served by a passenger train of some variety, but it was no secret that operating passenger service was rarely a profitable aspect of the railroad business. Railroads were often required by their public charters to provide passenger service, and the contracts for pulling the mail cars offset much of those operating costs.

Continuing its approach into Terminal Station, the *Nancy Hanks* passed two long thin buildings gridded with windows. They were built by the Southern Railway as an office building and freight depot in 1912, just south of the station. By 1928, much of the local freight distribution was already being moved outside of Downtown. The freight depot was converted to offices, and both buildings were expanded upward to eight stories each. The narrow ends of the two buildings were connected by a five-story enclosed bridge that arched above Nelson Street.

To facilitate the expansion of the yard trackage leading into Terminal Station and serving the freight depot, the city had allowed the Southern Railway to remove a short iron bridge at the Nelson Street crossing, provided that the railroad build a replacement spanning the expanded yard. The result of this unusual arrangement was that years later when the station was gone and the railroad relocated its offices to Midtown, neither the city nor the railroad was inclined to maintain it as a public right-of-way, and it fell into disrepair.

Finally the *Nancy Hanks* passed beneath Terminal Station, which was looking much less welcoming and more utilitarian from behind and below, before easing into its berth along the butterfly sheds and concrete platforms. After

The Spring Street viaduct is generally level, connecting
higher ground at Marietta Street and at the site of
Terminal Station. Warehouses lining the tracks continued
beneath the bridges. This building housed printing
facilities for the *Atlanta Journal-Constitution*.

four decades of heavy use, Terminal Station had endured some noticeable alterations by the late 1940s. The giant glass train shed had been dismantled after less than two decades, because it was difficult to maintain, having been replaced with the standard inverted butterfly sheds along the platforms between each pair of tracks. The two signature towers that flanked the station entrance had been significantly truncated, removing a level of open archways and decorative detailing, and making the overall appearance more austere.

Facing Terminal Station from across Spring Street, the Terminal Hotel prominently anchored a group of hotels along Mitchell Street that served travelers from the railroad station. By the 1940s, visitors were more likely to stay in the newer, larger hotels on Peachtree Street north of Five Points, such as the Henry Grady and Winecoff. Although Terminal Hotel burned to the ground (twice), a full block of buildings still stands on Mitchell Street in one of Atlanta's least known historic districts, Hotel Row, still largely awaiting preservation.

■

ALTHOUGH IT WOULD STILL BE DECADES before any civic space would be built above the Gulch as Bleckley had envisioned, beginning in 1928 the city undertook an ambitious project that would dramatically change the landscape of downtown. Three new concrete viaducts were built over the tracks east of Whitehall (now Peachtree) Street, at Pryor Street, Central Avenue, and Washington. At the same time, viaducts were added above the two streets parallel to the tracks, Wall Street to the north and Alabama Street to the south. The result was two full blocks of an elevated street grid, from Central Avenue to Whitehall Street.

The sidewalks of the viaducts were, in most cases, installed right up to the face of existing buildings, which were remodeled to put a new main entrance at the viaduct level. When new buildings were added, they were designed to seamlessly meet the elevated sidewalks, addressing that as the primary street entrance. With relatively few open vistas down to the tracks, the experience from street level was simply another low hill among many, such that it was difficult to discern when one was at grade and when one was on a bridge.

The original grid of city streets remained at grade underneath the viaducts, now identified as Lower Wall Street, Lower Alabama Street, and Lower Washington Street. The old storefronts lining these entirely enclosed, tunnel-like spaces became service delivery entrances, or were treated as basements.

The addition of the viaducts was not entirely seamless. The Washington Street bridge cut directly through the long, gabled roof of the Georgia Railroad's freight depot, rather than crossing above it, requiring two new parapets on either side of the street to mend the hole (the eastern end of the building was later removed, and the western parapet now forms the end of the freight depot). The western end of Alabama Street, which had sloped upward to Whitehall, was excavated down several feet to maintain clearance beneath the viaduct, exposing the rubble basement walls of a few buildings into Lower Alabama Street. The Central Avenue viaduct was realigned to the west, to allow one lane to branch off from the base of the bridge at grade. This required the removal of approximately thirty feet from the end of Union Station, and the construction of a new east wall. In that process, the Zero Milepost, which had been within the northeast corner of the station, was exposed directly beneath the Central Avenue viaduct, without moving at all. Within just a few years, the obsolete second Union Station was torn down entirely, and replaced with a parking deck aligned to the Wall Street viaduct, further

adding to the continuity of the illusion of the elevated streetscape above, and concealing the historic ground below.

The aging second Union Station, having been indecorously stripped of its end walls and corner towers in later years, was replaced in 1930 by a third iteration two blocks to the west. The replacement was modest in size compared to Terminal Station. The head house was a simple neoclassical building whose primary feature was a monumental entryway with two short wings. Passengers arriving and departing passed through a two-story portico consisting of pairs of round concrete columns capped by a triangular pediment. It was also built at the elevated street level facing Forsyth Street, directly above the NC&StL tracks, with several stairwells leading down to platforms along six parallel tracks curving northward. Another road bridge connected between Forsyth and Spring Streets right alongside the station, and provided a shortcut for cabs transferring travelers between there and Terminal Station. That bridge and the rest of the depot have long since disappeared, but the concrete pads for two of the station platforms remain to this day beneath several layers of parking structures. Not long after completion of the third Union Station, its predecessor was dismantled.

A platform was constructed directly above the railroad tracks, in an irregularly shaped space facing Whitehall Street and diagonally across from the Peachtree Arcade, to create Plaza Park. It was the first city park and greenspace in Downtown since State Square, a tree-lined park that was next to the Union Depot until the Civil War. At the opening of Plaza Park in 1949, Mayor William B. Hartsfield dedicated it to "Atlanta's women, and children, the tired worker, and the weary visitor." Plaza Park contained just a few triangles of grass with modest plantings, framed by wide concrete walkways that radiated from a small circular fountain, framed by a delicate canopy. The clean lines of the modern composition were incongruously juxtaposed with its nearest neighbor, the dark, elaborate bulk of the old Kimball House hotel. The other side of the park formed a pedestrian-only street called Plaza Way, lined by a row of small commercial buildings. Along one side ran a series of circular benches with concrete canopies. These mushroom-like objects had tubular funnels in their core, following the diagonal line of the tracks below, and actually served to evacuate the smoke exhausted from steam locomotives passing below. Park visitors could watch the progress of a train below as puffs of black smoke were emitted successively by each funnel in the line.

The only greenspace in downtown, Plaza Park offered a spot for shoppers to rest and for office workers to eat lunch. Although its design implied a space of repose rather than activity, the park later gained a reputation as a gathering place for civic protests. The park was entirely rebuilt in 1987 when Underground Atlanta was developed as a mall. Two small retail buildings, often vacant, occupy the corners, making it feel much less like a public park. Where the line of shops once stood, a cascading fountain (following the diagonal line of the tracks below) and monumental steps lead down to the new entrance of the mall. It has been supplanted by nearby Woodruff Park as a weekday respite, but draws large crowds every New Year's Eve for the annual Peach Drop celebration.

In the days before chain stores and regional shopping malls, many people rode the *Nancy Hanks* into the city specifically to go shopping for the day. They might have gone to the Kress ten-cent store, still standing on what was Whitehall Street, or to the famous Peachtree Arcade, on the same street just at the north end of the viaduct. Inside an unassuming building, a long narrow atrium space was lined on both sides with shops on three levels. Cast iron columns and ornate railings framed the balconies, and a glass skylight bathed the entire space in daylight. But the primary shopping destination was typically Rich's Department Store, just blocks from both stations. It filled an impressive six-story building on Broad Street, designed in 1924 by premier Atlanta neoclassicist architect Philip Schutze. Founded in a small wooden storefront on Whitehall Street just after the Civil War, it had grown into a beloved institution, known for its fair business practices and generosity as much as for its broad selection of goods at affordable prices. They maintained a no-questions-asked return policy, and, in periodic economic downturns, they would accept credit or even barter in lieu of cash payment. When the city struggled to pay teachers during the Great Depression, Rich's arranged for them to be paid in script that was good for store credit. In addition to being a destination for household necessities, Rich's was seen as representing the core values of the New South: welcoming, trusting, forgiving, successful, and philanthropic.

In 1948 Rich's opened its expansive Store for Homes, a sleek International-Style steel and glass building with four floors of showrooms. It was just across the street from the newly completed offices of the *Atlanta Constitution* newspaper, a red brick edifice with a curved entry corner and tiered roof levels distinctive of the Streamline-Moderne architectural style, which somehow evoked the form of an ocean liner. An all-glass Crystal Bridge over Forsyth Street connected the Store for Homes to the main Rich's building. This became the location of a new holiday tradition, the annual lighting of the Great Tree. On the day after Thanksgiving, a sixty-foot pine tree mounted on top of the crystal bridge was lit, while choirs sang carols from each level of the glass bridge.

■

IN THE PERIOD WHEN RAIL TRAVEL WAS AT ITS PEAK, other competing modes of transportation were already arising that would completely redefine the

Passenger Train at Union Station, 1942.
Steam locomotive #514, a 2-8-0 Consolidation type, stands
with its train ready to depart from the third Union Station,
with a brakeman perched on the footboard. The scene is
viewed from directly beneath Spring Street, looking toward
the tall office buildings on Marietta Street at Five Points. The
steel-framed bridge was demolished at the same time as
the station, in 1971. COURTESY OF THE ATLANTA HISTORY CENTER.

urban structure of the city. As ubiquitous as the railroads had been in every aspect of life in the early twentieth century, their decline would forever change the face of nearly every city in America. The destruction of Pennsylvania Station in New York City is often credited as inspiring the birth of the modern preservation movement. The waiting halls modeled after the Roman baths at Caracalla, and the cathedral-like vaulted skylights supported by delicate exposed steel structure, were in the end no match for changing times and the pressures of real estate development. The architecture evoked the timelessness of great civic monuments, but it was only a commercial structure dedicated to a particular business. Likewise, the demolition of Terminal Station in 1972 struck a chord among those who had passed through it, mobilizing a preservation movement in Atlanta. Two years later, activists successfully campaigned to save the ornate Fox Theater from being torn down. The lavish theater was designed in an eclectic Moorish style by the same architectural firm that designed Terminal Station. Now fully restored, it is hard to imagine the city without this cultural centerpiece and architectural masterpiece. Many significant buildings have succumbed to the wrecking ball in Atlanta, but the loss of Terminal Station stands foremost in the regrets of those who knew it, even almost fifty years later.

Henry Ford had opened a Model T assembly plant on Ponce de Leon Avenue in 1915, signaling that times were changing. As automobiles became increasingly available to the middle class, they fed the all-American instincts for independence, adventure, and elbow room. As roads were improved beyond the city center, people could drive farther from their workplace to buy homes where lots were generous and inexpensive. Atlanta's extensive streetcar network carried fifty-seven million passengers in 1913, linking residential neighborhoods and commercial hubs. Streetcars carried workers to industrial sites like Inman Yards, and on weekends took families to Ponce

Springs and Grant Park's Lake Abana. But the entire network of tracks was removed in the 1950s, just as they were in most American cities.

Nothing symbolized the growth of suburban culture in Atlanta more than the opening of Lenox Square Shopping Center in 1958. Notably, it included the first suburban outposts of Rich's Department Store and its downtown rival, Davison's. Not only was it the first mall-style shopping center in the Southeast, but it was also the largest single development in Georgia. Its success signaled the dawn of a new type of satellite retail center, further diminishing the role of downtown in the lives of metro Atlantans.

The first Atlanta airplane flight took place in 1910, when daredevil aviator Charles "the Bird Man" Hamilton raced his plane against a car around the two-mile track at Candler Field as entertainment during an auto race. Hamilton lost, but by 1925 Candler Field, a racetrack built by Coca-Cola founder Asa Candler, had been converted to a landing stop for air mail service. In 1927, Charles Lindbergh landed his *Spirit of St. Louis* at Candler Field on a tour celebrating his solo flight across the Atlantic. Lindbergh, who had learned to fly in rural south Georgia, was paraded through town, drawing the largest public gathering in the city's history (until the 1939 premiere of *Gone with the Wind*). His message promoting the commercial potential of aviation, which until then had been viewed as a pastime for eccentrics and daredevils, was received well. A prominent street in the growing northern suburbs was named in his honor.

Led by future mayor William Hartsfield, the city employed some vision and self-promotion (both in abundance in Atlanta) to establish itself as a hub for air mail routes, being well positioned as a stopping point between Florida, the Gulf Coast, the Midwest, and the Eastern Seaboard. The city purchased Candler Field in 1929 as its municipal airport. American Airlines began operating scheduled passenger flights shortly thereafter. A new international terminal

———————————

Magnolia Street passing through the earthen embankment
supporting the Norfolk Southern tracks along what was
once Elliott Street. Light descends from an opening
in Andrew Young International Boulevard, which
otherwise encloses the space between State Farm
Arena and the Georgia World Congress Center.

Safety netting installed beneath the Washington Street viaduct because it was literally crumbling. Before it was replaced in 2018, signs warned pedestrians to watch for falling concrete debris.

was built in 1961, the largest single terminal in the country, with flower-like expressionist concrete concourses. The entire terminal was razed again in 1980, relocated and rebuilt many times larger into its current configuration. By 1957 it was the busiest airport in the country, and by the end of the century, Hartsfield-Jackson Atlanta International Airport had become the busiest airport in the world.

Massive investment at the state and federal levels on road infrastructure, including the interstate highway system, further encouraged the transition away from the railroads. The post office ended its RPO contracts in favor of air and truck delivery, contributing to the end of rail passenger service. Standardized shipping containers were adopted. Individual businesses no longer relied on access to their own railroad siding for deliveries. Instead, trains unloaded at large multimodal transfer facilities onto trucks, which covered the remaining miles to their destinations.

In 1971, most of the passenger rail service in the country was consolidated into the federally managed Amtrak. The Central of Georgia's *Nancy Hanks* had been reduced to a few cars that operated from a corner of the Southern Railway's office building on Spring Street. The Georgia Railroad continued to operate its last passenger trains #103 and #108 out of their office on Hunter Street near the State Capitol. These "super-mixed" trains consisted of a single passenger coach tacked onto a line of freight cars, which made regular stops en route to set out and pick up freight cars from industrial sidings, which certainly must have tried the patience of the few remaining passengers.

The *Nancy Hanks* made its last run on April 30, 1971, the day before Amtrak commenced operations. Atlanta was left with only one interstate passenger train, which took the name and route of the Southern Railway's *Crescent Limited*. The through-route from Washington, DC, to New Orleans ran on trackage connected through Howell Junction, and therefore did not enter the Gulch at all. Brookwood Station, a small but stately suburban depot designed by Neil Reid in 1918, four miles north of Five Points on Peachtree Street, was promoted to Atlanta's main passenger station. The great passenger terminals were left as obsolete relics of a way of life that had disappeared, anchors to a restless city that had long since moved on. Union Station was demolished in 1971, and Terminal Station followed a few months later. But within just a few years, civic leaders were working to bring passenger trains of a different sort back into the Gulch.

With continued expansion into suburbs and surrounding municipalities, and a combined population of over one million, it was clear that Atlanta had grown from a city to a metropolitan region. The Metropolitan Atlanta Rapid Transit Authority (MARTA) was formed by voter referendum to provide a modern subway system to move commuters through the city efficiently. But other than a four-mile stretch bored through solid granite directly beneath Peachtree Street, the route was mostly squeezed along the rights-of-way of existing railroads. The system initially consisted of two primary lines, one running east-west along the Georgia Railroad, the other north-south following the Southern Railroad and the Atlanta & West Point. These lines naturally intersected right in the Gulch, just between the sites of the former Union Stations, at a station on Peachtree Street named after the nearby Five Points intersection.

Passengers disembarking trains on the north/south platform ascend an escalator that dramatically punctures through a historic building façade. It belonged to the 1901 Eiseman Clothing building, one of the many buildings removed to clear space for the Five Points station. The five-story building was clad in a tan glazed brick, with large round-arched windows. It was topped with generous amounts of ornately sculpted terra-cotta, including a pair of

The tracks of CSX Transportation beneath the CNN Center.

half-nude female statuettes projecting from the face of the upper floors. Lamenting its fate, a preservation-minded architect on the design team for the station proposed that the sculptural elements be salvaged and incorporated into the interior of the station as part of MARTA's program of installing artwork or murals in each of its stations. The terra-cotta was meticulously

The modern depot built for the New Georgia Railroad directly beneath the Central Avenue viaduct at Lower Wall Street. The building was removed in 2019 to allow for the demolition and replacement of the viaduct. Prior to demolition, the Zero Milepost was removed to the Atlanta History Center, and a replica was later put in its place.

dismantled, and two of the upper floors of the façade were reassembled inside the station. Although rather incongruous with the station's modern design, the three large arcades of old windows perfectly frame the tracks below.

Construction of the Five Points MARTA Station, the centerpiece of the system, was disruptive to the area to say the least. Two full blocks of historic storefronts in Underground Atlanta, on the north side of Alabama Street, were demolished to make room for the new tracks approaching the station. Massive excavations for the station, underground tracks, and connecting tracks took out additional buildings on Broad Street, including the second building designed by architect I. M. Pei. Before the Five Points station was complete, service was inaugurated on the line to Decatur from the Georgia State station in 1979. For a short time, passengers could actually connect from MARTA trains to the Georgia Railroad's super-mixed trains #103 and #108 just a block away.

The system was contemporaneous with similar systems in San Francisco and Washington, DC. It still enjoys consistent ridership among commuters, has been generally well maintained, and benefits from a direct connection to the terminal building at Hartsfield-Jackson Atlanta International Airport. But until very recently, expansion of the system has been stymied by opposition from the surrounding suburban counties and reluctance by the overwhelmingly rural state legislature to allocate funding. Nevertheless, it remains a vital part of the daily life of the city. Although it may lack the excitement of the *Nancy Hanks* or the grandeur of Terminal Station, thousands of passengers continue to arrive and depart downtown by train every day through the Five Points MARTA station.

Aerial View of the Railroad Gulch, 1965.
The newly completed viaducts for Hunter Street (now Martin Luther King
Jr. Drive) and Techwood Drive (now Centennial Olympic Park Drive) are
boldly superimposed over the rail yards in this aerial photograph looking
to the east. The cylindrical coal-gas storage tank on the left is soon to be
the site of the Omni Coliseum. COURTESY OF THE ATLANTA HISTORY CENTER.

III DIVERSIONS
(1972–2019)

STEPPING ON TO THE WORLD'S LONGEST freestanding escalator, visitors to the Omni Complex were filled with anticipation. The air was chilled by the indoor ice-skating rink spread out below them, where unsteady southerners traced loops around the ice. The 196-foot-long escalator swept up five stories through an enormous enclosed atrium capped by an expansive skylight. The walls of the atrium were lined with windows from offices and hotel room balconies. At the top of the escalator was the world's largest indoor amusement park, the World of Sid and Marty Krofft.

The Krofft brothers had created the popular television shows *H.R. Pufnstuf* and *Land of the Lost*. Like those, their amusement park at the Omni Complex was uniquely creative, and more than a little unsettling. Those who visited during its brief operation consistently recall that the surreal circus-like atmosphere was bewildering and unapologetically psychedelic, probably less oriented to kids than to young adults under the influence of illegal substances. Visitors were met at the top of the escalator by an insistent mime and a host of other larger-than-life characters from misbegotten hallucinations. The centerpiece of the rather limited selection of rides was the Crystal Carousel, on which all of the animals were cast from transparent plastic. Another ride provided visitors the experience of being a pinball, which was perhaps more unsettling than thrilling. Riders sitting inside a silver sphere ricocheted through the lights and sounds of a larger-than-life pinball machine, cascading down five levels of the atrium. Atlantan Jamey Propst, who took his family downtown to visit the World of Sid and Marty Krofft, recalled that it was populated by an abundance of midgets, an intrusive mime, "and some poor fat guy dressed up in a hippopotamus suit." He believed if visitors had one lasting impression, "they'll remember that damned mime, because he was just so strange. He sort of got in your face and he just sort of bugged you . . . and he wouldn't leave."

The Omni Complex also offered after-hours entertainment at a restaurant and nightclub owned by Burt Reynolds. Burt's Place sported an illuminated dance floor with a colored-glass caricature of the mustachioed movie star. Several of Reynolds's films had been shot in Georgia, making it the third-ranking state in film production at the time, and laying the groundwork for the significant presence the film industry would have in Georgia forty years later.

Perhaps not surprisingly, the World of Sid and Marty Krofft closed its doors after only six months. Aside from its dubious entertainment value, the venue's biggest flaw had to be its location, on the older fringes of downtown, on the edge of the railroad gulch. Its limited attractions proved insufficient to draw families from the suburbs. Burt's Place closed after one year, although the space later housed a Broadway-themed cabaret called the Manhattan Yellow Pages.

For decades, families had been migrating to the ever-expanding suburbs. Retailers, offices, and services likewise dispersed among the population, as there was no longer a significant benefit to being physically clustered together at the city center. For those businesses that remained, their workforce was largely commuting each day from the suburbs. The aging stock of two-to-six-story commercial buildings became increasingly outdated. Work space was replaced and consolidated into modern high rise office towers that took up entire city blocks. The demand for surface parking was so high that it often made more sense to tear down the smaller buildings than to renovate or rebuild them.

By the late 1960s, the city was decimated. Where once there had been miles of continuous urban fabric, huge gaps opened up. There were few businesses, countless acres of surface parking, and not a tree in sight. After office hours and on weekends, it was even more vacant. Crime and homelessness increased, or at least became more visible because of the lack of any activity on the streets. Especially for those looking in from the distant suburbs, the impression was that Downtown was dirty and unsafe. There was little or no reason to come into the city if you didn't work there.

There had been a time when the urban challenge was that the sidewalks were packed with too many people. In his *Report to the City of Atlanta on a Plan for Local Transportation* of 1924, John Beeler proposed alleviating the congestion with an underground tunnel with moving sidewalks beneath Peachtree and Whitehall Streets. Instead of subway trains, the tubes would have contained a series of parallel articulated belts, each traveling at successively faster speeds. The slowest allowed people to step on and off, from which they could transfer onto the faster lanes. Elegantly outfitted passengers lounged on sofas anchored to the moving sidewalks. It resembled a Victorian version of a ride at Disney World more than it resembled any modern form of public transportation. The tunnels under Peachtree Street were never implemented; instead, the problem of congested sidewalks was eventually alleviated by simply making them into places where no one wanted to be.

It was in this environment that the architect John Portman began a series of projects that would turn the tide of investment and public sentiment toward Downtown. While he may be criticized by some architects and urbanists for destroying the character of Downtown, he can also be credited with saving it.

Portman leveraged the early success of the Atlanta Mart, a windowless box that provided showroom space for wholesale retailers, into the development of Peachtree Center. This was a collection of identical slender office towers clustered around a central courtyard, complemented by an upscale restaurant and a dinner theater. Emulating the urbanism of Rockefeller Center in New York City, Portman aspired to create a new pedestrian realm in the heart of the city. While traditionally buildings had pushed to the edge of the sidewalk in all directions, he left generous space for an open plaza with a sunken garden populated by sculptures and water features.

When John Portman unveiled the new Regency Hyatt House Hotel in 1967, it was like nothing anyone had seen before. He imagined a hotel that had been turned inside-out, or more accurately, outside-in. Four walls of guestrooms formed an interior courtyard twenty-two stories tall, with a roof of white glass and lush vines draping down from every balcony. Even the elevators were exposed, a kinetic sculpture lit up like Buck Rogers capsules zipping up and down through the center of the atrium.

The hotel's lobby was connected to the other public spaces of Peachtree Center by a series of tubular bridges. These provided convenience and air-conditioned comfort, but also emphasized the insular nature of this idealized pedestrian realm. Portman saw the public streets as little more than a

The World of Sid and Marty Krofft, 1976.
View from the top of the atrium at the center of the Omni
Complex. The World of Sid and Marty Krofft, which operated
for only six months, is already being dismantled. The world's
longest freestanding escalator now takes tourists to the
entrance of the CNN studios. COURTESY OF THE ASSOCIATED PRESS

utilitarian vehicular zone. In truth, there were not many streetside amenities left to engage by then. His buildings presented nothing but blank concrete walls to the street, punctuated by peekaboo entrances, *porte cocheres*, and gaping service bays. In an effort to alleviate people's fears, rational or otherwise, and draw them back downtown, he was creating indoor cities that, from the outside, looked and acted more like bunkers.

Portman's sensational design for the Regency Hyatt House has since been replicated around the world. It served as inspiration upon which the Omni Complex was directly modeled, with its lofty interior atrium enveloped by a windowless concrete exterior facing the street. Now that the streets surrounding the Omni Complex and Peachtree Center are once again bustling with shops and sidewalk cafes, efforts have been made to redesign the entrances and introduce street level windows. While they are responsible for drawing hundreds of thousands of people into Atlanta each year for business and tourism, the presence of the monolithic concrete boxes continues to interrupt the vitality of the pedestrian experience.

About the same time that Peachtree Center was being built, Georgia State University was expanding its campus near Hurt Park, just across the tracks from the Georgia Railroad Freight Depot. A series of classroom buildings was built around a small outdoor plaza, which was elevated with one level of parking below. Pedestrian bridges across Decatur Street connected it to other campus buildings, but access points to the public sidewalks below were limited, and to this day they are often blocked by locked gates. Like Portman's projects, the priority was to achieve a feeling of protection from the rest of the city. In an era of student protests, it was also advantageous that the student gathering space be in a highly controlled, sequestered environment. The first viaducts had been built to separate the city streets from the danger and

Passages between the buildings of Georgia State University, beneath the Washington Street viaduct. The subsurface zones are often used by students to come and go, but at other times, signs of human occupation are scarce.

obstruction of the railroads. This second generation of pedestrian bridges was intended to separate people from the perceived dangers of the public streets.

The Omni Complex was sited, in many people's opinions, on the wrong side of town. In 1967, the City of Atlanta had opened the Atlanta Civic Center, a forty-six-hundred-seat civic auditorium intended to host opera and Broadway productions, combined with a modest convention hall. It was located just north of Portman's expanding Peachtree Center, filling in a low-lying slum once known as Buttermilk Bottoms. When the state was considering sites for a new convention center, the favored solution was to build next to the Civic Center, with John Portman proposed as the architect and developer. This would have complemented the successful hotels and Merchandise Mart, and continued the growth of the business district northward along Peachtree Street toward Midtown. Winning such a large public project would have required a great deal of political savvy, but Portman, being a self-made man, bristled at the need to cozy up to politicians and was unable or unwilling to close the deal. In retrospect, the immensity of the current convention center would have obliterated the surrounding residential neighborhoods, and impeded any pedestrian continuity with Midtown.

Instead, an enterprising developer named Tom Cousins approached the State with a bold proposal of his own. In exchange for selecting him as the developer, he offered to donate twelve acres of land he owned at the opposite end of Downtown. His site lay on Marietta Street, the other major commercial street branching from Peachtree Street at Five Points. It was perched on the edge of the railroad tracks, overlooking the last vestiges of the passenger stations. Cousins had already gambled on the area on the outer reaches of the central business district, building a large parking deck with air rights he had secured over the platforms of Union Station. What he needed was an attraction to fill it with cars. The State accepted his offer, and the Georgia World Congress Center was born. Directly between his parking deck and the convention halls he created the Omni Complex. Opened in 1976, this combined the Omni International Hotel, offices, and shops within a single concrete megastructure, wrapped around an atrium that clearly emulated those of Portman's hotels. It was directly connected to the Omni Coliseum, built in 1972 for an NHL expansion team, the ironically named Atlanta Flames. As is often the case, its location had less to do with thoughtful urban planning, and more to do with where land could be assembled inexpensively by a developer willing to take a risk and make a deal. The hotels were supported by visitors attending conventions, but the entertainment venues were intended to be family-oriented destinations. Drawing families into the city proved to be a struggle for decades.

Once a thriving city neighborhood that hosted all the aspects of "live, work, and play," Downtown had been reduced to solely an environment for working. Reintroduction of the housing component was handicapped by banks that were notoriously reluctant to provide financing for new high rise apartments in the city. The entertainment venues were an effort to at least reintroduce the element of play into the district.

One family-oriented attraction that consistently drew people to the area was the Pink Pig ride at Rich's Department Store. The beloved ride was a train of cramped cage-like enclosed cars, with a pig's nose at the front and curly tail at the rear. The inverted monorail was initially suspended from the ceiling of the toy department, then in later years it was relocated onto the roof, its short loop offering dramatic skyline views. It remains an endearing holiday tradition, although it has since been replaced with a more banal train ride inside a large tent in the parking lot of Macy's at Lenox Mall.

Parking structure near the Dome/GWCC/
Philips Arena/CNN Center transit station

The convention center continued to expand over the years, and the Omni Coliseum became home to the Atlanta Hawks NBA team. It hosted the 1988 Democratic National Convention and countless memorable concerts. The Omni Complex was purchased by Ted Turner for the headquarters of his groundbreaking Cable News Network (CNN). The twenty-five-year-old Omni Coliseum was imploded in 1997 and replaced with Philips Arena, now named State Farm Arena, so that Turner could secure another NHL expansion team, the Thrashers. The team was not named for Cousin John Thrasher, whose Monroe Embankment lay buried directly beneath the ice, but instead for Georgia's state bird, a small brown bird that rustles around under bushes.

The former amusement park in the Omni became television studios from which the news was broadcast around the world, and a movie theater was added that played *Gone with the Wind* for years. The ice-skating rink has long-since been replaced by a food court, but the escalator still leads visitors up through the atrium to tours of the CNN studios.

The Omni, rebranded as the CNN center, remained awkwardly situated on the edge of Downtown, until a new city park was created in anticipation of the Centennial Olympic Games. Clearing away several low-density blocks that had been known for little more than auto repair shops, the park was intended to link the Convention Center, sports arenas, and the CNN Center with Peachtree Center and the hotels of Peachtree Street. The park came up to the front doors of the Omni, which was at long last at the center of a popular entertainment district. It was soon surrounded by more hotels, a children's museum, the College Football Hall of Fame, and a two-hundred-foot-tall Ferris wheel.

■

Down in Atlanta G.A.

Underneath the viaduct every day

Drinking corn and hollerin' hoo-ray

Pianos playin' till the break of day.

—"Preachin' the Blues," Bessie Smith, 1927

THE OLD SHOPFRONTS OF LOWER ALABAMA STREET, tucked beneath the elevated viaducts, had gained a reputation during Prohibition as a popular district for speakeasies. Just steps from the railroad tracks and the second Union Station, the district was nonetheless well hidden from public view. But after the repeal of the Eighteenth Amendment, the street fell back into disuse and was largely forgotten. It was by no means lost or sealed off, and some particularly adventurous residents recall making visits and finding a dark, dirty street lined with boarded up, deteriorating historic buildings. From the busy streets above, it was difficult to detect the extents of the "underground" streets below, which added to their mystique. The viaducts in most cases appeared to be a continuation of the naturally hilly topography. Over time, the exposed upper building facades were renovated or rede-signed as modern trends dictated, while the neglected lower level appeared frozen in time. Some buildings were demolished above the viaduct level but their bases remained, further exaggerating the disparity between the two aspects of the same street.

This forgotten district remained suspended in its abandoned state until two graduates from Georgia Tech, Steven Fuller and Jack Patterson, had a vision to make it come alive again. In 1969 they opened Underground Atlanta, an entertainment district filled with restaurants and bars, billed as a "city beneath the city." The vaguely nostalgia-themed establishments bore names like Muhlenbrink's Saloon, The Rustler's Den, The Bank Note, and the obligatory Scarlett O'Hara's. The atmosphere was deliberately evocative of Bourbon Street, with cobblestone streets, gas street lamps, narrow side-alleys, and cramped quarters. As a finishing touch, an old streetcar was placed at the entrance, peeking out from underneath Central Avenue.

This incarnation of Underground consisted primarily of a two-block length of Lower Alabama Street, lined with historic buildings on either side, with the underside of the city viaduct as its roof. In all, it included roughly sixty tenants in seventeen different buildings, many dating from the 1870s to 1890s. Some of the streets dead-ended where the viaduct above sloped back down to grade. Other streets crossed the railroad tracks at grade and connected back to the surface streets to the north. In this way, while it was secluded and covered, it was still open in several places to the other city streets.

Beneath Central Avenue, visitors could step across the rails and get their photo with the Zero Milepost, which had recently been exposed from within a pile of protective timbers, and given a historical marker. Other unusual venues included Josephine Tussaud's Wax Museum, with over one hundred wax figures on three floors; the Musical Museum and Arcade, home to Chico, the organ grinder monkey; and Gone With the Wits, a cabaret theater featuring the Wits End Players. A sailing ship hatchway in the sidewalk revealed stairs leading to Dante's Down the Hatch, a nautical-themed fondue restaurant in the guise of a pirate ship packed into a basement. A pool of water surrounding the stern of the ship was occupied by live alligators.

Underground Atlanta included a restaurant and souvenir shop operated by former governor Lester Maddox. He had become famous as proprietor of the Pickwick Restaurant near Georgia Tech, where he defended his segregationist principles by wielding axe handles to scare off black customers. After selling the Pickwick rather than giving in to integration, he ran for governor of Georgia in 1966. In an unlikely turn of events, he won despite not receiving the most votes in either the Democratic Party primary or the general election. Perhaps more surprisingly, his single term in office was largely without scandal, and included the adoption of integrationist policies. It was during his subsequent term serving as lieutenant governor for Jimmy Carter that he ran his souvenir shop in Underground Atlanta. It offered an array of politically themed memorabilia, along with miniature axe handles dubbed "Pickwick Sticks." A consummate self-promoter, if a little rough around the edges, Maddox performed in a musical comedy duo with a former busboy from the Pickwick, blues musician Bobby Sears. Calling themselves "The Governor and the Dishwasher," Maddox played harmonica and Sears played the guitar, interspersed with stilted banter in the manner of the Smothers Brothers. They performed their act every Saturday night at Underground, and toured the country, making appearances on the *Dick Cavett Show* and *Laugh-In*.

Aside from the eclectic location and nostalgic atmosphere, much of the success of Underground Atlanta must be attributed to an exemption it enjoyed from Georgia's alcohol laws. The sale of mixed drinks was forbidden throughout the state of Georgia, but Fulton County had passed an exemption that allowed the sale of so-called "liquor by the drink" in restaurants and bars, provided the customers adhered to a dress code of formal attire. But as neighboring counties relaxed their liquor laws as well, patronage at Underground declined. To compete, Fulton County removed the dress code clause, which opened the doors to all manner of clientele. As business declined, some establishments introduced striptease dancing. Nearly one-third of the district was demolished in 1975 to make way for a new MARTA right-of-way.

Behind the quaintness and patina, it was in the end a series of cramped bars and dark alleys that literally never saw the light of day. The vagrants that tend to populate the spaces under roadway bridges moved back in, and a few well-publicized muggings further discouraged suburbanites from making the trip into town. With declining attendance and a sharp increase in crime, Underground Atlanta was closed in 1980. David Goldfield summarized in his 1982 book *Cotton Fields and Skyscrapers* that "the only thing the entrepreneurs of Underground Atlanta proved was that with enough capital they could transform an old deteriorating area into a new deteriorating area."

Ten years later, a reborn Underground Atlanta was filled with thousands of people celebrating a victory that would mark a new stage in the growth of the city. At a ceremony in Tokyo on September 18, 1990, officials of the International Olympic Committee announced the selection of Atlanta as host city for the twenty-sixth Olympiad to be held in the summer of 1996. It was a dream that had been heavily promoted by Billy Payne, head of the Atlanta Committee for the Olympic Games, as well as Atlanta mayor and former UN ambassador Andrew Young. Just a few decades earlier, Atlanta had been just another city in the Deep South, comparable in size to Birmingham, Alabama, or Memphis, Tennessee. Now its business-friendly atmosphere, home to such Fortune 500 companies as Coca-Cola, Delta Airlines, and UPS, was attracting a more cosmopolitan population, and Atlanta was ready to make a name for itself internationally. Although not quite as precocious as when Knoxville, Tennessee, hosted the 1982 World's Fair, Atlanta was certainly the underdog competing in its bid for the Olympics against the cities of Athens, Melbourne, and Manchester, among others. But it was the perfect application of Atlanta's strengths: a unique mix of hospitality, optimism, guileless self-promotion,

Underground Atlanta, Lower Alabama Street, 1970.
Muhlenbrink's Saloon was one of the many bars and nightclubs
that made Underground Atlanta a popular destination in the
early 1970s. The cast iron storefront pre-existed the concrete
viaduct, which was built directly to the building face, fully
enclosing the street below. COURTESY OF THE ATLANTA HISTORY CENTER

unstoppable growth, and a penchant for deal-making, all packaged under the euphemism of "boosterism." It was a defining ethos that seemed to have been present since Stephen Long had first declaratively driven a stake into the ground, not far from where the crowd was gathered. This vibrant optimism, along with an unprecedented seven million dollars spent pursuing the bid, had persuaded the International Olympic Committee to believe in Atlanta. IOC officials were impressed by the city's strong economy, infrastructure, racial tolerance, and of course the potential American television audience. Upon hearing the news of the selection, former mayor Maynard Jackson proclaimed, "[I] never felt more elated in my entire life. I felt like an exclamation point has just been laid down in the line of our city."

Underground had been entirely redeveloped into a modern shopping mall in 1989. The new pedestrian plaza at the corner of Alabama and Peachtree Street had become the natural gathering place for city-wide celebrations. Every New Year's Eve, it hosted the Peach Drop, in which tens of thousands of partiers counted down to midnight while a giant peach descended a tower in the middle of the plaza.

Transforming the shuttered remains of Lower Alabama Street into a bustling destination had been a campaign promise of Mayor Andrew Young, to take advantage of the expanding convention traffic nearby. He crafted an aggressive deal in which the city bundled four blocks of buildings and leased them to the Rouse Company. Eighty percent of the $144 million development was funded from local, state, and federal resources. Eminent domain was implemented to transfer lots from 150 private owners to the Downtown Development Authority. Rouse had recently developed large tourist-oriented shopping malls that had helped spark the revitalization of waterfront districts in Baltimore, New Orleans, and Portland. Each city would also add a signature aquarium, a seemingly unavoidable trend Atlanta would come to late but, as usual, attempt to out-do all of its competitors.

The architectural character of the new Underground was considerably different from its previous incarnation, not just because of the boldness of the vision. While the deal was still being struck, a series of fires passed through the abandoned structures, destroying several buildings. When contractors later moved in to begin the work of renovation, at least one building is said to have collapsed as soon as it was touched. The most significant impact was caused by the construction of the MARTA line running east to Decatur alongside the right-of-way of the Georgia Railroad. Despite the number of tracks that had previously run through the site of Union Station, it was determined that the new electrified tracks had to be added to the south. This required the demolition of two blocks of historic buildings that had formed one entire side of Underground, including the towering Century Building.

The buildings that remained at this time were surveyed and placed on the National Register of Historic Places in 1978. Underground had been declared a local historic district by the city at the same time as the Martin Luther King historic district. However, when the city overhauled its historic preservation laws, the district was not reestablished. The newly created Urban Design Commission worked hard to save the Century Building, but without local designation, there was no review process in place to protect the historic buildings from alteration or demolition.

A significant number of changes were also required to upgrade the ad hoc collection of occupied storefronts and basements into a modern shopping mall. All the buildings had to be brought up to current building codes for construction and life safety, which was no small task. Accessibility standards for the mobility impaired required the installation of ramps and easily

Beneath Centennial Olympic Park Drive. Support structure for State Farm (formerly Philips) Arena, which replaced the Omni Coliseum. The steel truss allows the arena to span clear above a portion of the Dome/GWCC/Philips Arena/CNN Center station.

walkable surfaces. The streets were repaved with non-historic brick pavers. Walls of glass enclosed either end of Lower Alabama Street, so that the space under the viaduct could be air conditioned and locked after hours. A police precinct was included on site to manage concerns over safety and security. Two blocks of Upper Alabama Street above were blocked off for pedestrians only. To expediently evacuate smoke from the mall in the case of a fire, a series of mysterious white metal stacks populated the pedestrian street above, reminiscent of the smoke stacks from the original Plaza Park. The themed restaurants of Underground were replaced with a food court, national chain retailers, and a few bars. A burger joint resembling a 1950s malt shop was added where the old streetcar had been. Where buildings had been removed, replacement storefronts were added in a noticeably contemporary style, with some nod given to adjacent historic detailing.

Plaza Park was entirely rebuilt, with a cascading fountain and broad steps leading down from Peachtree Street to the new glass-walled entrance tucked beneath the viaduct. The end result was that it felt more like an indoor mall with historically themed shopfronts than a part of the city street grid. Two multistory parking decks were added along Martin Luther King Jr. Drive, occupying almost as much space as the mall itself.

The rejuvenated Underground Atlanta was initially very popular, attracting thirteen million visitors in its first year. Dante's Down the Hatch reopened, and in fact, it had been left completely intact since its last day of operation. For several years, the famous drag queen Charlie Brown headlined at a nightclub. A replica steam locomotive from a defunct amusement park was placed as signage near the Central Avenue entrance, with life-sized cartoon characters from the Warner Brothers Store climbing over it. It became the most visited tourist destination in the state, despite its waning amount of historic, cultural,

A MARTA train traveling westward from the Dome/
GWCC/Philips Arena/CNN Center station. The concrete
columns bear the platform for Georgia International
Plaza in front of Mercedes-Benz Stadium

or entertainment content. Other attractions opened nearby, increasing the draw to out-of-town tourists.

Next door to Underground, the World of Coca-Cola contained galleries of advertising memorabilia and the opportunity to sample variations of the soft drink from around the world. A three-story corporate gift shop in the guise of a museum, the World of Coca-Cola nonetheless celebrated one of the success stories of Atlanta, and a globally recognized brand. It quickly became the city's most-visited indoor attraction.

Beginning in 1986, visitors could once again board a steam-powered passenger train, near the site of the first Union Stations. The New Georgia Railroad pulled dinner trains past Decatur and looped around the foot of Stone Mountain. The trains were pulled by Atlanta & West Point 750, a 4-6-2 heavy Pacific steam locomotive restored to operation by volunteers of the Southeastern Railway Museum. More than a few heads must have been turned upon hearing the low whistle echoing through streets once more, or seeing plumes of black smoke drifting over the tree-topped neighborhoods. A small brick depot was built for the operation, directly underneath the Central Avenue viaduct. The building enclosed the long-neglected Zero Milepost, giving it a prominent place of display without moving it at all. The train ride was the pet project of Steve Polk, director of the Georgia Building Authority, mostly driven by his personal love of trains. Under Polk's direction, the state purchased the Georgia Railroad's old brick Freight Depot nearby, and restored it for use as an events facility. Built in 1869, it is the oldest building remaining in Downtown. The New Georgia Railroad operated for eight years until state funding was abruptly discontinued following Polk's death.

The advent of the Olympic Games transformed the Gulch, but not as much as it could have. The largest of the Olympic venues was the Georgia Dome, completed in 1992. It was built next to the expanding Georgia World Congress Center, on top of what had been the railroad yard of the Atlanta, Birmingham & Atlantic Railroad. The tent-like roof was covered with a translucent white material that glowed with daylight, supported by a complicated trusswork of cables and struts known as a tensegrity structure, the largest of its kind in the world. The seventy-one-thousand-seat facility was built as the new home for the NFL Falcons franchise, and during the Olympics hosted gymnastics and basketball events.

A massive parking structure was constructed in the space between the Georgia Dome and the Omni Complex, aligned with the level of the adjacent Techwood and International Boulevard viaducts. It sat at a low point in the natural topography, the deck extended eight stories below the entrances to the stadium and arena. The top level was filled with lawns, trees, water features, and sculptures, creating a pedestrian plaza along the lines of what Haralson Bleckley had envisioned ninety years before.

Other cities might have taken the opportunity to fill the vast empty spaces of the Gulch with a collection of other Olympic venues. But other host cities had also found that such monumental sites built specifically for the Olympics were difficult to make use of afterwards, leaving expansive unoccupied holes in the middle of a city. Atlanta's novel approach was to distribute the new venues across the entire metropolitan region, embedded in facilities that would be better suited to use them long term, resulting in the architectural legacy of the Olympics dissolving away quickly as facilities were modified or became better known for subsequent uses. The most lasting monument to the Games is Centennial Olympic Park, but instead of being built across the empty parking lots of the Gulch, where it could have connected the Dome, Omni, and GWCC to Five Points Marta Station, Underground Atlanta and the government buildings of South Downtown, it was instead located as a

The squat brick structure that was built as a depot for the New Georgia Railroad in 1986, viewed from Lower Wall Street. Built in place underneath the Central Avenue viaduct, it enclosed the W&A Zero Milepost, as well as several of the supporting columns of the bridge. After the tourist train ended operations, the building was used as an office and training room for the State Capitol Police. The building was demolished in 2018 in preparation for a project to rebuild the viaduct, at which time the Zero Milepost was removed and put on public display.

bridge between the Omni and GWCC to Peachtree Center and the hotels of Peachtree Street. The Gulch would remain relegated to surface parking and gameday tailgaters.

While MARTA rail expansion remained stifled for years by the fears of exurban residents in adjacent counties, the new transit aspiration lingering on the agenda of planners was the Multi-Modal Passenger Terminal. The "MMPT" was conceived as a consolidated terminal for Amtrak trains, inter-city buses, and a proposed system of suburban commuter trains, all integrated with the Five Points hub of the MARTA rail network. For many this was clearly derived from a desire to replicate the former passenger train terminals as a monumental point of arrival in downtown. Glamorous renderings were released to the public every few years, each more extravagant than the last. The heart of the MMPT concept was the commuter trains, which would utilize the existing railroad corridors branching out in all directions. These would connect to the suburbs beyond the reasonable reach of the electrified MARTA trains, to all the communities from which people commute into the city for work each day, thus alleviating daily commuter congestion on the freeways. Such systems are integral components of the urban infrastructure in New York, Chicago, and San Francisco. Negotiating the right to operate passenger trains on the private freight railroads is complex, but not impossible. The suburban communities had all grown up around railroad depots to begin with. The confluence of these proposed lines remained at the junction in the railroad gulch.

A concentrated effort was made by some legislators and citizen support organizations to initiate a first leg of such a system. Federal funds were earmarked for a line to the southeast, and CSX, having acquired multiple parallel routes through various mergers, agreed to lease an underutilized redundant rail line. Unfortunately, the project never accumulated enough support

Union Station Demolition, 1971.

The third Union Station, located on Forsyth Street, was demolished in 1971, just months before Terminal Station met the same fate. That same year, Amtrak began operating the Southern Crescent out of the Peachtree Station in Buckhead, along a through-route that did not pass through the Gulch at all. The last passenger trains serving downtown, the Georgia Railroad's mixed trains #103 and #108, ceased operations in 1983. COURTESY OF THE ATLANTA HISTORY CENTER.

among state legislators, the majority of whom represented rural communities far from Atlanta. After nearly two decades, the federal funds were rescinded, and CSX, enjoying ever-increasing demand, withdrew its offer and reactivated the line for freight service.

Not only did this dramatically limit the transit goals for metropolitan Atlanta, it also suspended the potential redevelopment of the Gulch as a passenger rail terminal. Oddly, proposals for the MMPT persisted. The city had purchased the old *Atlanta Constitution* newspaper building across the street from the Five Points station, but suspended in a derelict condition it only served as a highly visible monument to inaction. Any possibility of Amtrak passing through the Gulch again was eliminated when the route of the Richmond & Danville Railroad was developed into the highly popular Eastside Beltline trail. Without Amtrak or commuter rail, the MMPT would be little more than an overblown bus station, hardly living up to its original vision of a grand entry point to the city.

■

PEOPLE STOOD IN THE AISLES OF THE HEARING CHAMBER for the City Council meeting on November 5, 2018, and more watched the proceedings on televisions from two additional overflow rooms nearby. After months of deliberation, a vote was expected to determine the fate of a massive development deal between the City of Atlanta and a real estate investment group called CIM. If approved, the proposal would fill a majority of the open area of the Gulch with dozens of buildings, interconnecting streets, and greenspace. The five-billion-dollar project would be the largest development since Peachtree Center, filling the "barren pit" with nine million square feet of office space, one thousand residences, plus hotels and retail space. The forty-acre site included eighteen parcels with nine skyscrapers, all built on platforms to the level of the existing viaducts. To close the deal, the city would commit nearly two billion dollars in public funding over thirty years, the largest public investment in the city's history.

The deal was being championed by the new mayor, Keisha Lance Bottoms, but had met with unanticipated skepticism from the City Council. With seven newly elected members, the council wanted to show that it was no longer a rubber-stamp for the mayor's agenda, after the previous mayor Kasim Reed had railroaded through a number of similar deals with little public support. Three times, the City Council had declined to vote on the proposal, asking for more information or more time to deliberate. Suddenly the Gulch went from being an obscure collection of parking lots to being at the center of public discourse. An aggressive promotional campaign to "Green-Light the Gulch" included automated phone calls and radio ads, and filled residents' mailboxes with glossy fliers packed with statistics and artists' renderings. Bright green T-shirts were handed out to supporters at the meeting, while those opposed wore red. They had been left frustrated by the single public information session, in which only a few preselected comments were addressed. They were arguing for more transparency and public input than what had been conducted by Mayor Reed for the sale of Underground Atlanta.

Despite its popularity, the revamped Underground had proved economically unsustainable, losing $8 million in its first five years of operation. It even lost $6.5 million in 1996, the year of the Summer Olympics. Full of commercialized nostalgia but lacking authentic historical substance, it did not compare well with similar "festival marketplaces" in other cities. The opening of the world's largest aquarium in 2005 secured the area surrounding Centennial Olympic Park as the new primary tourist destination. Two years later, the

Near the Washington Street viaduct, students enter the
classroom buildings of Georgia State University from one level
up, and the space below is dedicated to services and parking.

World of Coca-Cola was relocated across from the park, and the building next to Underground was shuttered. Other new attractions were added around Centennial Olympic Park, drawing more tourist traffic away from Underground. Major retailers left, and while it still drew crowds on weekends, its character changed as the clientele shifted from tourists to local residents. It slowly succumbed to the cycle of declining attendance and loss of tenants that has led to the death of malls across the country.

Mayor Reed became convinced that the city needed to divest itself of Underground Atlanta, riddled with vacancies and struggling with falling attendance. He found an interested buyer named WRS, and argued that the city should be grateful for their offer. A public request for proposals was issued, but with such an unreasonably short deadline that no other developer responded. Given that the property consisted of dozens of consolidated acres of real estate sandwiched between Five Points, Georgia State University, and the government center, it is likely that a more open process would have yielded a number of attractive offers. WRS had a portfolio of suburban strip malls and big-box stores, but had no experience qualifying them for this particular type of project. But, they did promise to inject a healthy mix of housing, retail, entertainment, and a supermarket into a part of downtown that desperately needed it. The few conceptual renderings they released suggested a skillful understanding of urban richness. The scope of their redesign was such that it was never clear what their intent was for the actual "Underground" portion of Lower Alabama Street. In public statements they claimed to be committed to saving as much as possible, but preservationists pointed out that they were not beholden to save anything. Because the city had never reestablished the local historic district designation, the few historic elements that remained had no legal protection against demolition.

The City Council was urged to approve the deal quickly, lest the opportunity not come again. The effort to obtain public input had been negligible. As a further means to close the deal, Reed negotiated a land swap in which the pastoral Bobby Jones Golf Course was given to the State of Georgia in exchange for the plot of land where the first and second Union Stations had stood so many years ago. That land was subsequently sold to WRS, possibly to offer more parking to potential supermarket tenants, which further disappointed those hoping for urban density there. The sale included the Alabama Street viaduct, which had already been a pedestrian mall, and the enclosed space below. Oddly, this also necessitated the abandonment of portions of the active cross streets, Pryor Street and Central Avenue, where they crossed over Lower Alabama. Citizens concerned about the sale of public land to a private developer were further upset about relinquishing the public domain of busy sidewalks into private control. The deal was approved, and Underground closed its doors once again in 2017. But WRS has struggled to get financing or tenants for the ambitious project, which is a challenge even for those well versed in urban redevelopment sites. Years later, the mall remains closed except for a popular music venue that has relocated to a historic warehouse in the rear.

Meanwhile, a group of German investors called Newport, teamed with local developers, had quietly acquired a collection of over four dozen individual buildings and parcels just southwest of Underground. South Downtown, walled off by railroads on two sides and interstate freeways on the others, had floundered in recent years while other parts of town experienced rapid growth. The neighborhood includes an admirable collection of small-scale historic commercial buildings with eclectic styling representing a range of decades, abandoned or under-utilized, amid a patchwork of surface parking lots. But the streets are unsettlingly quiet, despite several large government

Nelson Street, passing between the ends of the two
Southern Railway office buildings. Mercedes-Benz Stadium,
with its iconic geometry, was completed in 2018.

office buildings filled with hundreds of workers daily, who are adamantly ensconced behind security checkpoints.

WRS relies on the contemporary model of assembling large tracts of real estate to accommodate big-box retail tenants with ample parking. In contrast, Newport aims to address the district as a whole, rejuvenating existing properties one at a time. This incremental approach has the potential to produce a more thoughtful mix of small-scale urban infill and historic preservation. It also takes more time, and years later they have produced little more than excitement and attractive renderings.

The first significant project to move ahead in the area was headed by CIM. Their initial venture into the Gulch was to purchase the two Southern Railroad office buildings along Spring Street, which loom over the west edge of South Downtown, to be renovated as apartments. The ends of the two buildings are connected by a multi-story enclosed bridge that arches across Nelson Street. The Nelson Street bridge, still owned by the railroad, was deteriorating with neglect, and had long since been closed to traffic. Following negotiations with the developer and the city, the railroad planned to remove and replace the bridge.

The small brick interlocking tower remained standing next to the graceful arches of the Nelson Street bridge. Utterly obsolete, the South Tower had survived the demolition of Terminal Station, and stood empty beside the busy tracks of the Norfolk Southern for another four and a half decades. Across the country, most interlocking towers were torn down, and a few have been preserved as museums, while the South Tower was simply ignored. In 2007, the Atlanta Preservation Center included the tower on its list of Ten Most Endangered properties, recognizing that its continued existence was largely an accident, and that without proactive effort, it could be lost at any time. Being perennially overlooked was simultaneously its salvation and its greatest threat.

A similar brick interlocking tower survived at Chattanooga Terminal Station, which had been restored as a hotel, complete with passenger cars converted to sleeping rooms. But a new hotel owner bulldozed the Chattanooga tower in 2017 despite public protest, to make way for new luxury housing.

With the sale of the adjacent land to CIM, and anticipating the replacement of the Nelson Street bridge, the Norfolk Southern determined that it was finally time to remove the South Tower. Just months after the Chattanooga tower fell, the 117-year-old South Tower was bulldozed without any public notice or review. Preservationists and nearby residents had hoped that it could have been repurposed as a small retail amenity linking the neighborhoods on either side of the bridge, and complementing the historic railroad office buildings and warehouses. Representatives of Norfolk Southern said they had looked internally at retaining or relocating the building and determined it was not feasible, but also acknowledged that they had not reached out to any other parties. They explained that the demolition of the tower was ostensibly to make way for a maintenance access road along the tracks.

Those who spoke against the Gulch deal were not opposed to developing the Gulch, but insisted that such a significant project be conducted with more planning, more public input, and fewer taxpayer dollars. No one was arguing that the Gulch should be left as is, although not all were convinced that the need to fill it was the most pressing need for the city, and that it could not wait for an offer to be presented that did not require so many public incentives to proceed. They called for a legally binding Community Benefits Agreement, dedicating funds to help adjacent low-income neighborhoods. They were concerned that financing the project with bonds secured from a tax allocation district would actually divert future tax dollars from local schools. They believed that public money should be spent on public infrastructure, rather than handing it over to private ownership. Like the development at

Far beneath the Georgia World Congress Center near
Magnolia Street, this geometric composition of concrete
columns appears thoughtfully intentional, despite the
unlikelihood that it would ever be encountered by a person.

Underground, new elevated platforms and connecting streets that would be built in the Gulch would fall into private ownership, largely because the city did not want the responsibility of maintenance and security, but also because it allowed a level of control over the environment that would promote the affluent, gentrified tourist-friendly vision. In Atlanta, the homeless themselves have no power and few advocates, but the irrational fears they instill have a surprisingly powerful sway on public and private policy. Opponents argued that streets are a vital part of the public domain, accommodating basic civil liberties such as gathering, protests, or just doing whatever you like. Anyone who has settled into a street-side plaza in front of a corporate office building and been asked by a private security officer to move along has become more aware of this distinction. They advocated for a more aggressive commitment to support affordable housing, in a city in which the lack of low-income housing was reaching critical proportions. Significantly, they pointed out that the deal should include requirements that the platform structures and parking decks be planned to allow expansion tracks for a multimodal commuter rail terminal to be installed at some point in the future.

In an op-ed column, urban critic Maria Saporta wrote: "Creating an architecturally elegant Grand Central Station for Atlanta . . . would give the project great historical context, reminding everyone of the special significance of that site. In short, including a multimodal station—one that would serve commuter trains, intercity trains, long-distance buses and other modes of transportation—would give the CIM-Gulch development a soul."

The supposed need for quick action was influenced by two Fortune 500 companies that were planning to relocate their corporate headquarters at the time. Retail behemoth Amazon was conducting a secretive but highly publicized search for a city in which to locate a second headquarters. Atlanta was believed to be on a short list of cities that were scrambling to compete for a reported fifty thousand skilled jobs. Proposals to Amazon were not made public, but it was evident from the scope and timing that the mayor and CIM were intending to tailor the Gulch development to accommodate Amazon.

It was a plausible scenario. Companies in the high-tech sector employ a younger workforce that prefers a more urban environment. The Gulch site offered plenty of space for a large corporate campus built from scratch, a downtown location, direct access to transit, relatively affordable single-family housing in close proximity, several nearby universities from which to draw new talent, and convenient access to the airport. This attractive combination would certainly be difficult to find in any other city. But just weeks after the Gulch vote, it was revealed that Atlanta had lost out to far more trendy venues in Arlington, Virginia, and Queens, New York. In contrast to Atlanta, residents and local politicians in Queens were so critical of the potential downsides of the massive development that Amazon was convinced to withdraw their plans to expand there.

The Norfolk Southern Railroad, successor of the Southern Railroad, was also considering moving its main headquarters out of Norfolk, Virginia, to Atlanta. They declared that their relocation to a new $575 million campus in Midtown was contingent upon the sale of their land within the Gulch to CIM. The actual connection between the two contingencies was not clear, but as a negotiating tactic, it did put more pressure on City Council to make a decision.

The weeks of debate over the Gulch redevelopment had not yielded much change in the proposal, and the politicians were getting anxious to reach a conclusion. After six hours of public comment and deliberation until near midnight, the City Council approved the deal much as it had been originally proposed. The Norfolk Southern did confirm the relocation of its headquarters to Midtown shortly after.. The Gulch will once again be transformed, although it is still largely left to speculation as to what form it will take, or when. Immediately after the vote, the mayor addressed the members of City Council with a quote borrowed from Nelson Mandela: "It always seems impossible until it is done." "And over the past few months, at times it has seemed impossible," the *Atlanta Journal-Constitution* quoted the mayor as saying, "But . . . we are here today. I do trust history will be kind to us, and we will be judged on how we leave this city."

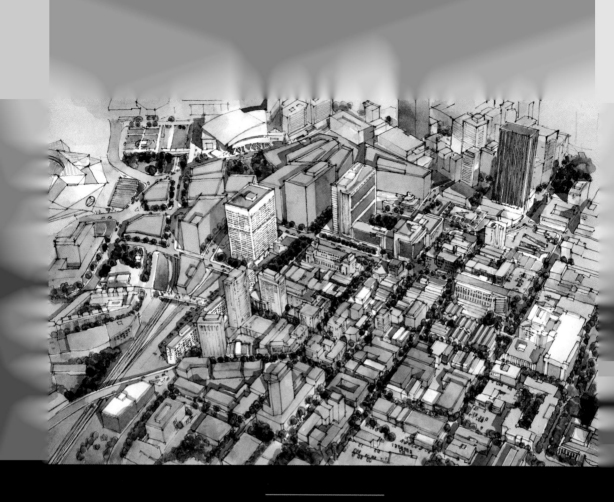

Proposed Redevelopment of South Downtown, 2019.
Conceptual rendering by Newport illustrating the potential redevelopment
of South Downtown with renovations and small-scale infill projects on
individual parcels. Newport has acquired over 85 percent of the private
land in the neighborhood. To the west (left) is Castleberry Hill and
Mercedes-Benz Stadium, to the north (top) is State Farm Arena and the
Marietta Street corridor. Larger buildings and a number of new street
connections are shown filling in the Gulch, although the area is being
planned separately by the CIM Group. COURTESY OF NEWPORT US RE

IV RESURGENS

THERE IS AN UNSETTLING MOBILITY TO THE MONUMENTS HERE. What isn't lost to the wrecking ball is uprooted or displaced by the best of intentions. Of those that have been relocated, the most well traveled is probably the statue of Samuel Spencer.

A native of Columbus, Georgia, Spencer became the first president of the Southern Railway, assembled from the Richmond & Danville Railroad and the East Tennessee, Virginia & Georgia Railroad. He was killed shortly after the completion of Terminal Station when his private car became uncoupled en route and was crushed by a following train. Thirty thousand employees of the Southern Railway contributed funds to erect a memorial in the fore-court of Terminal Station. In a departure from traditional heroic poses, he was depicted seated solemnly in a large armchair, atop a stone base designed by architect William White. The sculptor Daniel Chester French would repeat this approach later for the colossal figure of Abraham Lincoln in his iconic seated pose in the Lincoln Memorial. Spencer was positioned with his back to the street, his gaze fixed upon the station, greeting visitors upon their arrival. The statue was flanked by four ornate cast bronze lampposts, each borne on the shells of humble tortoises.

When Terminal Station was demolished, the statue was relocated to a tiny garden beside Peachtree Station, from which Amtrak had begun operating the *Southern Crescent*. After two decades there, it was moved to a small triangular park named for Hardy Ivy, at the point where West Peachtree branches from Peachtree Street. Those streets had once been relocated as well. Long before it was paved, Peachtree Street had originally continued straight down a hill and through a perennially muddy gully. The name was swapped with the diverging street so that Peachtree Street could retain the high ground. The triangle had at one time been home to the Judge Erskine Memorial Fountain, the city's first public fountain, donated to the city by his daughter in 1896. The fountain was later moved to Grant Park overlooking the picturesque Lake Abana, which has been filled in with a zoo, and the fountain has been largely neglected by the city ever since.

The statue of Spencer was joined at Hardy Ivy Park by the Carnegie Pavilion, a small arcade assembled from the remains of the Carnegie Library. The classical Carnegie Library was erected nearby on Forsyth Street in 1902 as a gift from Andrew Carnegie to the citizens of Atlanta. To the lingering regret of local preservationists, it was demolished in 1977 to make way for the new Central Library, which was a looming composition of concrete boxes that would be the final commission of Hungarian-born architect Marcel Breuer. After being discarded in a field for fifteen years, some of the carved stones from the Carnegie Library's exterior were cleverly reassembled by architect Henri Jova in a new configuration as a square open-air pavilion in preparation for the 1996 Olympics.

Most recently, Spencer was again moved three miles farther north on Peachtree Street and placed in front of the offices of the Norfolk Southern Railroad, a modern conglomeration built from the former Southern Railway. Remarkably, the four tortoise-borne lampposts are still beside him, having followed every step of his journey. Norfolk Southern is currently constructing their new corporate headquarters in Midtown, making it likely that Mr. Spencer has yet another move in store.

Just across the street from where Mr. Spencer had presided over Terminal Station, another statue towered over the corner of Hunter Street (renamed Martin Luther King Jr. Drive) and Spring Street (now Ted Turner Drive). The bronze sculpture designed by James Seigler depicts a woman, her arms outstretched, being lifted by a phoenix with its wings spread wide. Donated to the city by Rich's Department Store in 1981 in celebration of their one-hundred-year anniversary, it is titled *Atlanta from the Ashes*. After Rich's departed Downtown, *Atlanta from the Ashes* was moved across the Gulch to a corner of Woodruff Park at the busy Five Points intersection. The park itself, on land donated by former Coca-Cola president Robert Woodruff, had displaced two busy commercial blocks along Peachtree Street.

From Woodruff Park, the statue faces the restored Olympia Building, atop which is mounted a thirty-three-foot diameter sign advertising Coca-Cola in red neon. This red pinwheel-patterned "neon spectacular" is a 2003 re-creation of a sign originally installed from 1948 to 1981 in front of the offices of Coca-Cola in the ornately carved Candler Building. After that it was suspended high above the entrance to the World of Coca-Cola near Underground until that relocated to Centennial Olympic Park.

At the other end of Lower Alabama Street from the World of Coke, a single gas lamppost stood inside Underground Atlanta. One of fifty gas street lamps installed in 1855 by the Atlanta Gas Light Company, it attained

distinction during the siege of Atlanta, when a shell ricocheted off the base of the lamppost and killed African-American barber Solomon Luckie. The fractured lamppost became a symbol of the hardships endured by civilians during the bombardment. During celebrations for the world premiere of *Gone with the Wind* in 1939, it was anointed as "The Eternal Flame of the Confederacy." The lamppost had been displaced when Alabama Street was elevated, and later was moved back to Lower Alabama Street inside Underground Atlanta, within a few feet of its original location. Lastly, when Underground closed its doors for the second time, the lamppost was moved to the Atlanta History Center (AHC) in suburban Buckhead.

The History Center's research library contained a detailed reconstruction of the study of revered historian Franklin Garrett, including everything from books and photographs to furniture and paperweights. Mounted outside the entrance is a large round depiction of the state seal of Georgia. Rendered in terrazzo, the seal had been cast into the floor of the *Constitution* newspaper building in 1948. The building's Streamline-Moderne façade featured a seventy-two-foot-long bas-relief mural carved *in situ* by local sculptor Julian Harris, depicting various scenes from the history of journalism in the South, including manual printing presses, paper boys, and Brer Rabbit. The newspaper moved out only three years later after merging with the *Atlanta Journal*. When a new MARTA train station was built under the Omni Coliseum, the mural was removed and reinstalled above the escalators leading down to the train platforms. Nearby construction of the Five Points station was a massive undertaking that cleared several blocks of historic buildings near Underground. One of these, the Eiseman Building, was carefully dismantled and a portion of the façade was reassembled inside the station. The arched windows became tunnel portals for the tracks of the north-south line, making it the only building in Atlanta that is actually underground.

Through it all, the Zero Milepost remained in place, usually overlooked or out of sight. When the stone marker was originally installed in 1850, it stood just east of where the brick Union Depot was built four years later. This may have helped it survive the complete demolition of the depot by Union troops utilizing improvised battering rams. The second Union Station, with its larger footprint, was actually built around the milepost, which was described as being within the open-air area near the northeast corner of the depot. Near the end of its career, that end of the station was dismantled to make way for construction of the Central Avenue viaduct in 1929. The bridge, shifted north a few feet from the original street right-of-way, was constructed directly over the milepost in place. The stone was enclosed in a square cribbing of stacked railroad ties to protect it from the construction activity. The second Union Station was demolished shortly after the completion of the viaduct, and a few years later a single-level parking structure was built in its place. All the while, the milepost remained partially visible within its protective cribbing. In fact, it was not until 1958 that historians with the L&N, successor of the Western & Atlantic Railroad, made an effort to remove the ties and expose the milepost. An iron railing was installed around it, and a state historic marker explaining its significance was placed next to it. For twenty-seven years it could be found like that, next to a parking lot under a bridge, by anyone curious enough or brave enough to go looking for it. Visitors to the first iteration of Underground could simply walk across the tracks and have their picture taken with it.

In 1985 the New Georgia Railroad built a small depot on the site, utilizing the state-owned land of the old depot site and an unused siding along the Georgia Railroad. The red-brick building with a pitched roof was curiously built directly beneath the Central Avenue viaduct. An interior door off the lobby revealed a concrete bridge column occupying the back of a closet. The

exterior walls of the station were built around the milepost without disturbing it, leaving the stone as a feature within the central space of the depot. When the New Georgia Railroad ceased operations in 1993, the building remained under the ownership of the state. It was occupied as a substation and training center for the State Capitol police force, and the milepost could be accessed on weekdays by those who knew exactly how to find it. During the recession, the police station was shuttered, and the milepost was once again hidden from public view.

In 2018, as part of its systematic replacement of all the viaducts, the state Department of Transportation announced its plans to rebuild the Central Avenue bridge. The Georgia Building Authority (GBA), which managed the depot building, announced that it would need to be demolished at some time prior to the bridge replacement project. Fittingly, one of the arguments posed for clearing the site was to regain access to an adjacent parking garage, which would be temporarily inconvenienced by the bridge construction project. The irony, or tragedy, of displacing the milepost for the sake of a parking garage driveway was apparently not evident to the agency: history displaced for access to a parking deck. The GBA acknowledged that it was time to make a plan for the future of the milepost. Unfortunately, the agency did not exhibit the funding, creativity, or inclination to pursue an appropriate solution itself. It was also free from any requirements for public engagement that might have generated more creative solutions contributed by outside parties.

The GBA stated that it was committed to finding a solution by which the marker could be made accessible to the public while being protected from potential vandalism. Concerned citizens advocated that the milepost be preserved in place at all costs, because its inherent historic importance was derived from the exact location that it marked. The primary significance of the milepost was its location, marking the very birthplace of the city, and undisturbed ever since.

The agency deliberated behind closed doors, without public engagement, not responding to queries from the press. Then on October 29, 2018, the Atlanta History Center tweeted a video of the exhumed mile marker stone, wrapped like a cadaver, being wheeled into their new exhibition space. They announced that they had come to an agreement with the GBA to remove the milepost for display at their campus. The Atlanta History Center was willing and able to preserve and display the artifact, augmented with explanatory information. It was to be presented "in context" alongside the gas lamppost removed from Lower Alabama Street. Central to the new exhibit was the restored Texas locomotive, participant in the Great Locomotive Chase, also recently relocated from the basement of the Cyclorama in Grant Park. The lease agreement between the GBA and AHC contained an agreement of non-disclosure until the marker had been relocated, revealing their concern over public reaction. The public was shocked. A post by the Unseen Underground Walking Tour simply stated, "After one hundred sixty-eight years, the Zero Milepost no longer marks the endpoint of the Western & Atlantic Railroad and the original center point of our city. Having survived the Civil War, General Sherman, the construction of three depots and a bridge around it, and the demolition of two of those, it could not survive the best intentions of the Atlanta History Center, or the short-sightedness of the Georgia Building Authority."

Within a few weeks, the depot site was cleared as if it had never existed. The Atlanta History Center installed a freshly carved stone replica in place of the original and a bronze historical marker with amended text.

■

AS GENERAL SHERMAN WAS PREPARING TO EMBARK on his March to the Sea after occupying Atlanta for seventy-three days, he issued the fateful order that all structures of military significance be destroyed. This included all railroads, factories, and commercial buildings of possible use to the Confederacy. When soldiers liberally expanded this directive, burning all manner of homes and businesses, he made no effort to curtail them. The few civilians who remained in the city were terrified. When troops arrived at the Immaculate Conception Church, one block south of the Union Car Shed, they faced a fiery Irish pastor, Father Thomas O'Reilly. Father O'Reilly had opened his church as an infirmary during the battles for Atlanta. He personally pulled wounded soldiers from both sides of the battlefield to the church sanctuary, where Confederate and Union soldiers lay side by side as he cared for them, regardless of the color of their uniforms. In the months of the occupation, he had gained the respect of General Slocum and many Union soldiers, a considerable number of whom were Irish Americans.

Father O'Reilly declared that the burning of the city was a sin, and demanded that none of the churches be destroyed. He threatened the excommunication of any Catholic soldier who carried out such orders. At the encouragement of General Slocum, and in a rare display of compassion, General Sherman posted guards to defend the Immaculate Conception Church, as well as the nearby St. Phillips Episcopal, Second Baptist, Central Presbyterian, and Trinity Methodist, and also the combined City Hall and County Courthouse. To ensure that flames did not spread to the churches, no adjacent structures were allowed to be ignited either. As a result, a significant portion of the city was still standing when residents began to return. In fact, despite the powerful mythology, no more than 40 percent of the city was destroyed.

Father O'Reilly is still remembered as a hero for saving the churches and City Hall, and for his lesson in humanity, bravery, and compassion. But the

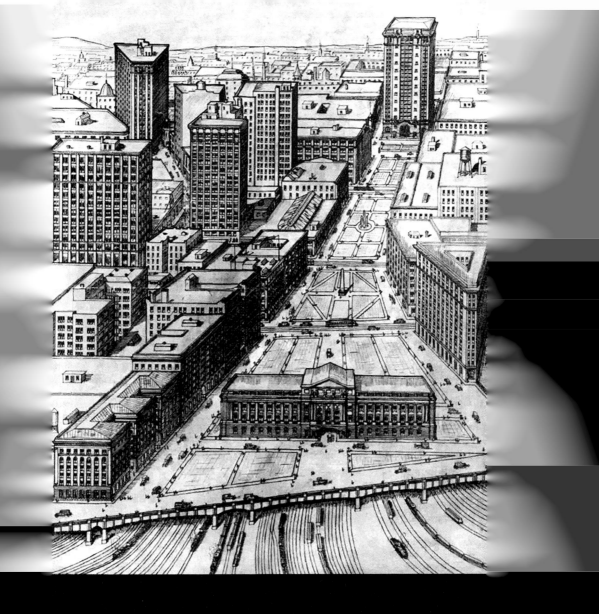

Proposed Civic Plaza, Haralson Bleckley, 1909.
...ezoidal building in the upper left is the Hurt Building, still standing, and the linear ...
Peachtree Arcade is visible along the plaza. Otherwise, the majority of the buildin...
...ous. Framing the plaza in the foreground is a conceptualized modern train station, ...
the third Union Station would be built several decades later. Tracks emerge from b...
...... Street, curving outward in the shape of the junction. COURTESY OF THE ATLANTA HISTORY ...

more relevant lesson may be the part of the story which is often overlooked, which is that not one of the buildings he saved remains standing today. Within twenty years of the Civil War, each had been torn down or replaced voluntarily. Immaculate Conception and Central Presbyterian were both replaced with larger sanctuaries. The other churches relocated to more residential neighborhoods to the north. New buildings were constructed for City Hall and the Fulton County Courthouse when Atlanta was designated as the state capital in 1868, and the small hill where they had stood became the site for the new statehouse. All of those institutions continue to thrive to this day, but none of the original buildings saved by Father Thomas O'Reilly still stand. In fact, of all of the buildings that were still standing within the city limits when General Sherman departed, not a single one survives. And yet, the story that endures in the minds of Atlantans is of how Father O'Reilly saved the churches from the wanton destruction of the invading northerners.

Atlanta's relationship to the past is strained at best. The city exhibits what may be a pathological compulsion to systematically erase its own history. Even when open space and surface parking abounds, it seems historic buildings are targeted for demolition to make space for new ones. Of course, this oversimplifies the limitations of site development that motivate property owners on a case-by-case basis, but the perceived trend is overwhelming.

The city's motto is "*Resurgens*," or "rising again," represented by the phoenix rising from the ashes. Much of the destruction during the Civil War was defensively self-imposed. After more than 150 years, the city is still rising from the ashes of its own self-destruction, shedding the past to face the future. Perhaps the burning of the city and subsequent reconstruction after the Civil War was so scarring to the collective psyche that ever since, building for the future requires the destruction of the past. Every new development, to be considered progressive, must first destroy something from the past. Our city

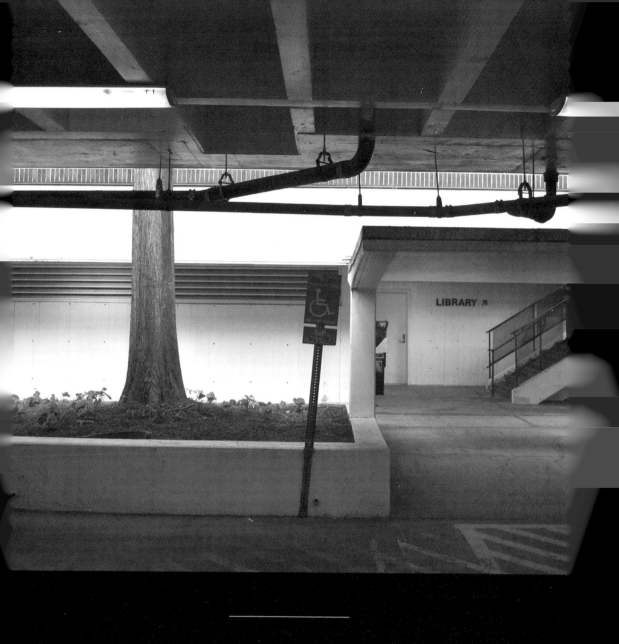

Stairs lead to the Georgia State University library building,
where cypress trees shade the student courtyard above.

is by nature always growing, and will always be tearing down the old to make room for the new, even when there is plenty of room for both. Take, for example, Hartsfield-Jackson Atlanta International Airport, which is consistently ranked as the busiest in the world. Its current capacity and efficiency were only achievable because twice in its history, instead of expanding or renovating, the entire facility was razed and rebuilt from scratch. Nothing is too bold to envision, and nothing is too precious to sacrifice.

When Arthur Blank proposed to build a new football and soccer stadium with over one billion dollars of his own money, a site was selected in the Gulch right next to the Georgia Dome, convenient to two MARTA stations and surrounded by parking. Unfortunately, two historic African-American churches would have to be removed to accommodate its footprint. Friendship Baptist Church was founded in 1862 by former slaves congregating in an empty boxcar. Spelman College began in the basement of the church's first building, which was also an early home for Atlanta University and Morehouse College. The hundred-year-old Mount Vernon Baptist Church had already been forced to move once in its history, for the construction of the Techwood viaduct in 1960, now Centennial Olympic Park Drive.

The stakes were clear: the professional sports venue, with its groundbreaking futuristic design, backed by a billionaire and promoted by all the politicians, against the small, African-American, private nonprofit institutions. To the city's credit, the use of eminent domain was never threatened. Preservationists, historians, and activists could voice their opinions but ultimately had little impact as outsiders. The decision was left to the individual congregations, and in the end they decided to sell for a combined thirty-four million dollars from the city and Georgia World Congress Center. Both buildings were demolished in 2014, and the stadium construction proceeded immediately thereafter. Perhaps they determined that their churches were more meaningful than just the building or land, perhaps they saw the good that could be rendered by such a monetary windfall, perhaps they recognized that the public momentum was behind the new stadium, and they made a commitment to move toward a new future for themselves. Mount Vernon Baptist Church relocated seven miles to the west, and lost some older members, but used the proceeds to further their mission. Friendship Baptist Church built a new sanctuary just a block away, with plans to reinvest in the community with a thirteen-acre mixed-use development, including a grocery store and mixed-income housing. They declared, "We are a church, not a building."

The phoenix also symbolizes that Atlanta is a city of transformation and rebirth. Exponential growth has been a defining characteristic since its inception, which suggests that it has always been largely made up of inhabitants who have immigrated from elsewhere. It is a city of people who have come here to start a new life. By necessity or by choice, they have left everything behind, sacrificed the husks of their own past to make way for the possibilities of a bold future. Even Scarlett O'Hara, Margaret Mitchell's metaphor for the city's coming-of-age, is torn between where she came from and where she is going. Her name evokes both the red earth of Georgia and her Irish immigrant heritage. Her refrain of "tomorrow is another day" is not so much a mantra of optimism, as it is a survival technique to forget. It is a means to repress the tragedies of yesterday, to live in denial of the challenges of today, and instead focus on the task of rebuilding tomorrow. This relentless commitment to looking forward rather than backward may be what defines Atlanta's relationship to the past. This is the heart of our city, and the source of our prosperity. Should we wonder that our physical environment is treated the same?

■

Magnolia Street, beneath the viaduct for Andrew Young
International Boulevard. The expansive stairs serve emergency
exits from the convention halls of the Georgia World Congress
Center. They imply crowds, but are never occupied.

THE ATALANTA OF GREEK MYTHOLOGY WAS ABANDONED on a mountaintop by her father, King Iasus, who had desired a son. As an infant she was suckled by wild bears, and then raised in the woods by hunters. She grew into a cunning huntress and brave warrior, fighting alongside the Argonauts as their equal. She refused to take a husband, pledging her virginity to the goddess Artemis. Those who attempted to ravish her were vanquished, among them two cyclops.

When Atalanta was reunited with her father, he persistently urged her to marry. She acquiesced on the sole condition that she would marry any suitor who could best her in a footrace; those who failed would give their life. Many men died this way, until Aphrodite intervened on behalf of Hippomenes, giving him three golden apples. During his race with Atalanta, he rolled the irresistible apples across her path and she could not help but follow them. Hippomenes won the race and they were married, but the brief marriage did not end well. They offended Zeus by making love inside his temple, and so he turned them both into lions, never to be together again.

Although it is entirely coincidental, the tale of Atalanta is an apt metaphor for the City of Atlanta. Born alone in the wilderness, she became fiercely independent, bold, and fearless. And she ultimately met her downfall by being distracted by shiny objects tossed in her path. In his 1903 essay, "Of the Wings of Atalanta" from *The Souls of Black Folk*, W. E. B. Du Bois declared, "If Atlanta be not named for Atalanta, she ought to have been." He argued that the rapid growth of Atlanta after the Civil War had promoted an overemphasis on wealth and materialism over the values of knowledge and culture.

Atlanta has historically been known for valuing aggressive deal-making rather than thoughtful design. Politicians have become more closely tied with developers, and electioneering has taken the place of planning. In recent years, the path to sound urban policies with a long-term vision has frequently been derailed by the pursuit of various legacy-making development deals. Beginning with hype and spectacular promises, they seem designed more to elevate certain politicians and corporations than to solve systemic problems with the urban infrastructure.

Certain characteristics of the Atlanta ethos seem to have been present since its inception, and persisted in each generation regardless of changing times and populations. These would include its reputation for gracious hospitality, innovation, boosterism, ambition, precociousness, and business savvy. Each trait has been evident in the institutions that occupied the Gulch: the Zero Milepost, the passenger depots, the Kimball House, Rich's Department Store, Underground Atlanta, the *Atlanta Constitution* and *Journal*, Friendship Baptist Church, and the Georgia Dome.

But more recent visions for utilizing the Gulch exhibit newer tendencies that alter the public trajectory. An expectation has grown through the last century that the city, state, and federal government should be proactively engaged in improving the built environment of the city. This began reasonably enough with the viaducts that provided safe passage across the busy railroad tracks, or the respite of Plaza Park that encouraged visits to downtown shops and businesses. In time the urban ails of the Gulch became more challenging, and the interventions grew larger and more radical. The Gulch and its environs have been the grounds for a number of ambitious new proposals in recent years, some hypothetical and some that may yet come to fruition.

Now, partnerships between public entities and private developers have become the expectation for large urban redevelopment projects. The public entity provides vision and represents the will of the people, supplemented by generous tax incentives, while the inclusion of a private party illustrates a commitment to free enterprise, distributes jobs and profits among the private sector, and offsets some of the financial burden from taxpayers.

Old Magnolia Street, facing the Georgia World Congress Center. The ramp leads to an intermediate level roadway that once served the Omni Coliseum, later covered by Andrew Young International Boulevard above.

The history of publicly funded ventures intended to promote local businesses ranged from the Cotton States and International Exposition to the 1996 Olympic Games. And of course the city began with the Western & Atlantic Railroad, an enterprise of the State of Georgia intended to promote commercial development. The Georgia World Congress Center, which operates nearly four million square feet of convention halls, is owned and operated by a state authority. It generates revenue for the state, but its real purpose is the financial impact it generates by drawing over three million visitors per year to the city.

By the end of the twentieth century, the land surrounding the Gulch was almost exclusively dedicated to public institutions of some form. The private businesses that once thrived along the Gulch are all gone. Rich's Department Store vacated its flagship location, and even the *Atlanta Journal-Constitution* moved its reporters and printing presses to cheaper real estate outside the city. With few exceptions, the immediate neighbors are now all government entities, including the Fulton County Courthouse and Georgia State University. State offices now occupy the former First National Bank tower, which was the tallest building in the Southeast when it was completed in 1966. Federal courthouses and government offices occupy three entire blocks on the south edge of the Gulch. The Richard B. Russell Tower stands on the site of Terminal Station, the former US Post Office now houses the Government Services Administration, and the Sam Nunn Atlanta Federal Center fills the two blocks once occupied by Rich's.

The original privately owned Underground Atlanta ultimately failed due to a number of forces beyond its control: liquor laws in adjacent counties, changing clientele, and security of the public streets. Subsequent endeavors, including the reincarnation of Underground, took advantage of public/private collaborative arrangements to specifically establish a controlled environment. Utilizing a large component of public funding stabilized the economic risks, and established certainty regarding permitting, licensing, and policing. Transferring the formerly public streets to private control, by literally walling them off with glass doors that locked every night, gave the private operators discretion over who came and went, and when.

The second iteration of Underground required significant public financing, as well as a controversial implementation of public domain seizures. This level of environmental control was noticeably different to patrons from the carefree nature of the previous Underground, and in the end failed to ensure either financial security or public safety.

Atlanta Beltline Green Necklace, 2015.
Bird's-eye rendering depicting the Atlanta Beltline as a "green necklace" encircling the city. The envisioned twenty-two-mile loop will be an assemblage of five railroad lines that bypassed the junction in the Gulch, transformed into a linear park linking dozens of neighborhoods.
(REPRODUCED WITH PERMISSION FROM ATLANTA BELTLINE, INC.)

Disoriented tourists and frustrated residents often complain that solutions to urban problems, whether large or small, that are obvious to them are not implemented. While grand unified visions like Bleckley's are compelling, the reality of urban planning is messy. As hard as it can be to create a grand urban vision, that is nothing compared with what it takes to implement it.

Unfortunately, planners usually make bad politicians, and politicians make lousy planners, and their areas of expertise have little overlap. The typical project is a complex interplay of politics, finance, public relations, and property rights, in which compromise is mandatory and design is a luxury. Well-designed projects with a clear powerful message are often the most likely to generate broad public support. But the obstacles of fractured land ownership, multiple diverse constituencies, and of course funding, rarely leave such a plan intact. As the public jurisdiction over the area has grown, so has the responsibility to ensure the success of any intervention. As the scale of public urban projects grows, so does the risk of failure. Like Atalanta, by chasing each new tantalizing proposal, we could lose our way entirely.

■

ATLANTA IS, IN MANY WAYS, A CITY OF GAPS. The urban fabric is plagued by discontinuities large and small that prevent it from thriving as a healthy, cohesive whole. In the mid twentieth century, aging building stock was razed rather than being renovated or replaced, and acres of surface parking took its place. Interstate freeways obliterated entire neighborhoods, and barricaded others. Other menacing obstacles include sports stadiums, corporate plazas, windowless megastructures, and empty blocks left fallow where crumbling housing projects have been cleared away. Against this decay, the city struggles to hold itself together.

The Gulch is one such gap, but it is not quite an empty hole. It is still an active railroad junction with long freight trains regularly thundering through. It teems with life on game days, blanketed with boisterous tailgaters. And it resonates with a history and significance that predates the city itself. Not merely an empty void, it is a particular place that has always been integral to the vitality of the city, though not particularly hospitable to inhabit.

It is not so much a hole that needs to be filled, as it is a wound in need of suture. This is a location fundamental to the creation and sustenance of our city, but in its current neglected state, it is one of our most challenging gaps. This is our own dry riverbed. Where other cities have leveraged their rivers as a resource to revitalize adjacent historic and industrial districts, we are left with the Gulch and the lingering question of what to do with it.

Atlanta has always had a peculiar relationship to its river. It breaks the pattern of most cities before it, which traditionally were established at seaports or river landings. The Chattahoochee River is roughly eight miles from Downtown, awkwardly distant, and even now that the metropolis has expanded well beyond its banks, it remains overlooked and underutilized.

In Chattanooga, our sister at the other end of the Western & Atlantic, the destination for the railroad was Ross's Landing on the Tennessee River, the obvious nexus of commerce and transportation. At this end of the railroad, however, the Chattahoochee River was viewed from the start only as an obstacle to be crossed. The railroad's objective was to bridge across the river, continue past, and there to join with two other railroads from across the state.

Both rivers are interrupted periodically by rocky shoals. In the nineteenth century, paddle-wheeled steamboats were hauled in to Chattanooga to operate over a portion of the Tennessee River, until eventually a system of locks and dams built by the Tennessee Valley Authority enabled continuous navigation. The Chattahoochee, being shallower and more frequently blocked by shoals, is entirely un-navigable above the Fall Line at Columbus, Georgia, and has never been of any use for transportation.

Nevertheless, local waterways played a significant role in the early settlement of the region. Fort Peachtree, the first government presence in the area, was built in 1814 on the promontory of land at the confluence of Peachtree Creek and the Chattahoochee River (now the site of a pumping station for the Atlanta Water Works). The first wagon roads were cut through the wilderness leading to mills built along creeks and rivers, or to places conducive to crossing by ferry, bridge, or ford. Those roads were given names still familiar to us today, such as Paces Ferry, Moore's Mill, Holcomb Bridge, and Rocky Ford.

By the time of the Civil War, stationary steam engines had replaced water wheels as the source of powering mills and factories, so being located near a railroad or a town became more important than being near a body of water. The impressive water-powered New Manchester mill on Sweetwater Creek, southwest of Atlanta, produced cotton for Confederate uniforms until it was destroyed during the Atlanta Campaign. After the war, the entire town was abandoned as obsolete, and has since reverted to forest around the ruins of the brick mill.

In more typical American waterfront cities, the business district developed along the water's edge, the point of arrival and departure for people as well as goods. Factories and rail yards lined the banks to gain access to the river. Through the course of the twentieth century, the dependence upon rivers for shipping and transportation was largely replaced by railroads, which in turn gradually gave way to interstate freeways and air travel. The general decline of heavy industries left massive industrial sites abandoned and decaying along polluted waterways that were neglected and inaccessible.

Mercedes-Benz Stadium viewed from Mangum Street.
The curved edge of the plaza above marks the hole
left by the recently imploded Georgia Dome.

Chattanooga is a successful example of a city that eventually rediscovered its waterfront as an asset. Water pollution was addressed, banks were cleaned up, and contaminated industrial sites were restored. Previously overgrown in-between spaces were developed as pockets of nature preserve and park space that reestablished access to the river for recreation and views. The adjacent historic downtown was given new life, offering density and character that paired with the natural amenity of the river.

Instead of evolving along the banks of the Chattahoochee, the business district in Atlanta grew tightly on either side of the rail junction, for proximity to the passenger and freight depots. The tracks were lined with warehouses and railroad facilities, the city incinerator, and a pair of enormous coal-gas storage tanks. Where other cities built bridges across their rivers, Atlanta built bridges across the increasingly dense rail yards in the center of town, in an effort to stitch together the busy streets on either side. As the tracks multiplied, more bridges were built, creating an elevated street grid that could function independently with few connections to the level below. The industrialized railroad yards became completely disconnected from the everyday city street life. Dirty, dangerous, and largely inaccessible to the public, the sunken area beneath the viaducts felt like a dry gully dividing the city. This was further exaggerated as the railroad facilities were demolished and replaced with fields of parking.

The area was never literally a gulch, but it did originally have more topography, including the upper headwaters of Proctor Creek. Low-lying terrain was incrementally filled in to accommodate expansion of the railroad yards. Natural streams were replaced by storm drains and underground pipes. As was common throughout Downtown, these were typically combined with sewer drainage, essentially converting the network of natural creeks into the city sewer system. Only recently has the city been going to great lengths to separate the two again. In the Old Fourth Ward, Clear Creek was daylighted from its underground culverts and became the centerpiece of a new park now surrounded by unprecedented development.

The Gulch is our dry riverbed. But despite the parallels, it cannot be rejuvenated in the same way. Other cities have had railroad yards in the center of town, and some dealt with them in similar fashion, but most had successful riverfronts as well. We have tried inserting new attractions into it: two or three versions of Underground Atlanta, the Omni Complex and its indoor amusement park, a sprawling convention center, two football stadiums, and arenas for basketball and two departed ice hockey teams. Despite their massive scale, none of these could adequately fill the gap. They either didn't generate enough sustained activity, or were not meaningfully connected to the rest of Downtown, or they required acres of surrounding land to remain as parking to support them.

Whether it is seen as an opportunity or a hole, there are many who recognize that the Gulch is at the heart of our city. This dry riverbed can somehow be nurtured back to life as a vital asset to the city. But if not as a river, then as what? It is more than just another brownfield site, like Atlantic Station, where the toxic residue of the past is literally sealed underground by a four-foot-thick concrete cap. It will not be sufficient to fill it with layers of concrete parking and spread a grid of anonymous mid-rise buildings across the top. We must come to know this as a place with history and memory and identity. It can only be brought back to life if we understand something about who we are and what makes us unique. Without such an understanding, any structures that fill the Gulch will remain hollow and meaningless.

Nearby, Bellwood Quarry is a literal hole in the ground of immense proportions. The abandoned quarry is being filled with water to create a reservoir for drinking water, and the surrounding leftover post-industrial space is becoming an instant waterfront park. It has amused some to imagine the Gulch, or even the Downtown Connector, being flooded to create a vast new water feature for the city. But if it is to be redeveloped, the Gulch must be much more than that.

The Atlanta Beltline exemplifies how such abandoned industrial infrastructure can be transformed into a revitalizing agent. An aggregation of five different railroad spurs that bypassed the downtown junction, it is envisioned as a twenty-two-mile loop of parks, trails, and transit. Where the railroad corridors lined with light industrial sites had once separated neighborhoods, the popular trail has triggered residential development to bind those communities together. What had been forgotten space is now a defining urban destination.

There is an opportunity to define a place, to make it what we idealistically want it to be. It could be a place that acknowledges its history, and explores the unique layering of the viaducts. It could be an integration of public city streets that celebrate the distinctive geometries of the railroad wye. It could be a neighborhood that reaches out to South Downtown, Five Points, Castleberry Hill, Vine City, the stadiums and Georgia World Congress Center, Georgia State University, Marietta Street, and the government district. It could be a community comprised of a diversity of people, jobs, and incomes, with buildings with a diversity of use, character, and ownership, in scales both grand and human. It can include a new passenger rail terminal, once again becoming a destination for thousands of daily commuters. It can be honest and inspiring, a generator, a focus, a real place, and a community.

Atlanta is a city of transformation and rebirth. The Gulch is no longer an obstacle to be overcome. It is an opportunity to be embraced, a door to be opened. This is not some vast pothole to be filled with more concrete. It is an opening to become whatever we can dream up.

■

THE SUBJECT MATTER OF THIS BOOK TOUCHES ON several atrocities that were committed during the brief history of our state: namely, the genocide of the Creek and Cherokee Indians; slavery and Jim Crow; crimes committed by both sides during the Civil War; and the subjugation of women's rights. It is not the intent to ignore, omit, or make light of these tragedies. It is, however, well beyond the abilities of this humble author to adequately address them, other than to acknowledge the debt we owe to those who have suffered before us. The lesson of history is that we owe our futures to the sacrifices, made willingly or not, of those who have come before us.

This is not a comprehensive history of Atlanta. It is a collection of stories specific to this small but significant area presented from a particular point of view. It is a narrative of the edges, both physical and conceptual, where the city and railroad junction are interconnected, from their inception and into the foreseeable future. The accounting of all that has been lost can be overwhelming, but while I always advocate for historic preservation, this is not intended as a reprimand. I only advocate that we know ourselves. Part of that is being aware of our complex and fascinating history, and part of that is acknowledging that we are a city committed above all else to building a better future.

ACKNOWLEDGMENTS

I am indebted to my family and friends for their patience and encouragement throughout the creation of this material. I must recognize the tireless work of Greg Germani to populate the Atlanta Time Machine website with countless then-and-now images. His work has inspired myself and many other amateur historians to take a second look at our surroundings and delve deeply into the fascinating history of our city. I would like to acknowledge the Atlanta Preservation Center, Central Atlanta Progress, and ThreadATL for being great supporters of the Unseen Underground walking tour over the years, and for their unflagging advocacy of preservation and urbanism. Special thanks go to my editors at Globe Pequot, the knowledgeable Kyle Kessler, and my sister Bethany Morrison for their insightful editorial guidance. Above all, I must express my utmost gratitude to all those who have attended my walking tours, for sharing their enthusiasm and curiosity, and often their own personal stories of this unique place. Without your support and inspiration, this book would not have been possible.

Magnolia Street passing beneath the Norfolk Southern Railroad, through
the embankment built by the East Tennessee, Virginia and Georgia Railroad
along Elliott Street. Andrew Young International Boulevard parallels Magnolia
Street far above, punctuated by circular openings in the median.

BIBLIOGRAPHY

Buffington, Perry, and Kim Underwood. *Archival Atlanta: Electric Street Dummies, the Great Stonehenge Explosion, Nerve Tonics, and Bovine Laws: Forgotten Facts and Well-Kept Secrets from Our City's Past.* Atlanta: Peachtree Publishers, 1996.

Cook Jr., Rodney Mims. *Atlanta's Parks and Monuments.* Charleston, SC: Arcadia Publishing, 2013.

Dooley, Laurel-Ann. *Wicked Atlanta: The Sordid Side of Peach City History.* Charleston, SC: The History Press, Arcadia Publishing, 2014.

Du Bois, W.E.B. *The Souls of Black Folk.* Chicago: A.C. McClurg & Co., 1903.

Faulk, Paul. *Trackside Around Atlanta 1956-1976 with Howard Robins.* Scotch Plains, NJ: Morning Sun Books, 2004.

Garrett, Franklin M. *Atlanta and Environs: A Chronicle of Its People and Events.* 3 vols. Athens: University of Georgia Press, 1969-1987.

Garrett, Franklin M. *Yesterday's Atlanta.* Miami: E. A. Seemann Publishing, 1974.

Goldfield, David. *Cotton Fields and Skyscrapers: Southern City and Region, 1607-1980.* Baton Rouge: Louisiana State University Press, 1982.

Inscoe, John C. *The Civil War in Georgia, A New Georgia Encyclopedia Companion.* Athens: University of Georgia Press, 2011.

Kuhn, Clifford. *Living Atlanta: An Oral History of the City, 1914-1948.* Athens: Atlanta Historical Society, University of Georgia Press, 1990.

McKay, John. *It Happened in Atlanta: Remarkable Events That Shaped History.* Guilford, CT: Globe Pequot Press, 2011.

Newman, Harvey K. *Southern Hospitality: Tourism and the Growth of Atlanta*. Tuscaloosa: University of Alabama Press, 1999.

Rose, Michael. *Historic Photos of Atlanta*. Nashville: Turner Publishing, 2007.

Rose, Michael. *Lost Atlanta*. London: Atlanta History Center, Pavilion Books, 2015.

Roth, Darlene, and Ambrose, Andy. *Metropolitan Frontiers: A Short History of Atlanta*. Atlanta: Longstreet Press, 1996.

Steinberg, David, and the Staff of the Southeastern Railway Museum. *When Atlanta Took the Train*. Charleston, SC: Arcadia Publishing, 2018.

White, Max E. *The Archaeology and History of the Native Georgia Tribes*. Gainesville: University Press of Florida, 2005.

INDEX